# ANTI-INFLAMMATORY DIET

## LIVE PAIN FREE & HAPPY - BOOST IMMUNE SYSTEM, RESTORE HEALTH, & FEEL AMAZING

## Disclaimer Notice:

Please note the information contained within this document is for educational and entertainment purposes only. Every attempt has been made to provide accurate, up to date and reliable complete information. No warranties of any kind are expressed or implied. Readers acknowledge that the author is not engaging in the rendering of legal, financial, medical or professional advice.

By reading this document, the reader agrees that under no circumstances are we responsible for any losses, direct or indirect, which are incurred as a result of the use of information contained within this document, including, but not limited to, —errors, omissions, or inaccuracies.

# TABLE OF CONTENTS

# Introduction

Thank you for buying this book. Inside, you will learn what inflammation really means – more than just swollen joints and other body parts – and how it affects your health, what an anti-inflammatory diet looks like, what the best anti-inflammatory foods are and of course, delicious recipes to help not just get on an anti-inflammatory diet but stay on it to reap its benefits. As such, you'll definitely learn so much about this chronic condition that afflicts millions of people in the world today and you can reverse or prevent it.

First, we will go through a thorough examination of inflammation and the role that it plays in your body. We will discuss acute inflammation, which is your body's natural reaction to injury and a way for the body to heal, and chronic inflammation, which is much more of a concern from a medical perspective and is rarely a positive thing. We will look at how chronic inflammation can occur, and the types of medical conditions that it can cause or exacerbate.

Then we will get into the anti-inflammation diet itself. We will discuss the basics of dieting in general, and then learn about the Anti-Inflammatory Diet, its purpose, and tips that you can follow to make sure that you are giving your body the best opportunity to fight inflammation in your system. We will examine the many foods and supplements that have anti-inflammatory properties, which will give you a great head start on the Anti-Inflammatory Diet. We will also look at foods that should be avoided because of their tendency to cause or worsen inflammatory responses.

Next we will go through a wide variety of healthy and delicious recipes that are designed to incorporate the Anti-Inflammatory Diet. Starting a new nutritional plan is always a difficult prospect, and sticking to it can be just as hard. But the tips and tricks provided in this book, as well as the varied recipes, will get you well on your way to successfully implementing the Anti-Inflammatory Diet.

After the recipes, we will take a look at the role that exercise can play in both causing and fighting against inflammation, and then we will discuss the importance of rest and recuperation in protecting against chronic inflammation.

Once you have read through this book, you will have a thorough understanding of the Anti-Inflammatory Diet, its basic premises, what it involves, what foods you should eat and which you should avoid, and how to both exercise and rest in a way that will best allow your body to fight against chronic inflammation.

If you're ready to kick inflammation in the butt, turn the page and let's begin. I hope that you enjoy this book, and I am sure that you will find it to be a valuable resource.

# PART I:  ANTI-INFLAMMATORY DIET 101

# CHAPTER 1: WHAT IS INFLAMMATION?

Inflammation comes from the original Latin word "inflammo" that literally means "I set alight" or "I ignite". Our bodies' immune system uses inflammation as a relatively simple way of protecting us from injuries or sicknesses. How does it work?

Our bodies do this by kicking out harmful agents like damaged cells, pathogens and irritants. This is accomplished by your immune system, which involves blood vessels, immune cells, and molecular mediators working together. These components work together to remove whatever caused the initial damage to the cell and to clean out any dead cells and tissue. Then, it follows up by healing whatever damage was caused by those agents that it evicted. And this is a natural process that our bodies were programmed for by God or evolution (if you're atheist). As such, any inflammation is a good sign that our bodies are actually putting up a good fight on our behalf.

Inflammation is a generic response – meaning that it is experienced essentially the same anywhere in the body in response to any injury – and so is part of the human body's innate immunity. This is opposed to adaptive immunity, which happens in response to specific types of injuries or threats to the body.

Inflammation is very closely regulated by the body, because if there is too little then the damage will not be prevented and repaired, but if there is too much then the inflammation itself can cause too much tissue damage and compromise your body's immunity. And if the inflammation goes on for too long (i.e. chronic inflammation), then that can lead to certain diseases such as periodontitis, rheumatoid arthritis, hay fever, and possibly even cancer. Therefore it is very important that your body monitors the inflammation process to make sure that your body is being taken care of properly and thoroughly when an injury does occur.

While inflammation isn't the same as infection, it can be a cause of such. One clear distinction between inflammation and infection is that fungi, viruses and bacteria cause infection while inflammation is our bodies' response to infections. To put it in clearer terms, our damaged body tissues, infections and wounds will never have a chance to heal without inflammation.

It is important to keep in mind the difference between inflammation and infection, because aside from the fact that inflammation is usually a beneficial thing for our bodies, they also do not always go hand in hand. There are situations – such as certain trauma or atherosclerosis - where inflammation is not a result of any bacteria, fungus, or virus. There are also situations where an infection can occur and not cause inflammation; this is often seen in parasitosis, which is when a disease is transmitted by a parasite.

Whenever we experience swelling or inflammation, it's automatic for us to do something that will bring it down. Often times, we don't really understand that the swelling or inflammation is good because it signals that our bodies are on the way towards healing and restoration. While it's true that brining down inflammation is crucial in some situations, it isn't so in most normal cases. Therefore, we should think twice about trying to help bring inflammation down the next time, i.e., it's necessary for healing.

CHRONIC VS. ACUTE INFLAMMATION

When we talk about acute inflammation, we refer to the kind that starts out fast and quickly becomes more severe. In fact, symptoms will often start to appear within the first few hours of an injury or other trauma, if not within the first few minutes. Acute inflammation is your body's initial response to injury, and occurs through the process of your body moving around plasma and leukocytes from the blood into whichever tissue has been injured. This process involves several of your body's systems, including the immune system, the vascular system, and a variety of different kinds of cells within your body.

In most cases, the symptoms are observable for only a couple of days although it can continue for more than 7 days in some cases. Some instances or conditions that can lead to acute inflammation include skin cuts or scratches, sore throat, infected ingrown toenails, acute bronchitis, acute sinusitis, acute appendicitis and high intensity workouts. If the process goes smoothly, then the cause of the injury will be removed and the repair process will be started quickly.

If you want to be able to better identify acute inflammation symptoms, remember the acronym PRISH, which stands for Pain, Redness, Injury, Swelling and Heat. In medical terms, these are referred to by their Latin names of dolor, rubor, function laesa (loss of function/injury), tumor, and calor. The symptoms of dolor, calor, rubor, and tumor were first described by Aulus Cornelius Celsus, a Roman encyclopaedist who was well-known for his medical studies. Celsus' medical treatise, *De Medicina* (On Medicine), was published around 30 AD and detailed an extensive amount of scientific and medical knowledge resulting from Celsus' work, including information about the inflammatory reaction of the human body.

Celsus' work was built upon around 100 years later by Aelius Galenus, a Greek physician and surgeon who added the function laesa symptom to the list of signs of inflammation. It is remarkable that these scientists, working within the limits of both the knowledge and technology of their times, were able to identify the symptoms of inflammation which are what today's medical professionals still rely on today to determine that inflammation is occurring.

The heat and redness that occur are a result of an increase in blood flow to the inflamed site, while the swelling is caused by fluid accumulation in the injured area. The pain occurs due to the release of chemicals like histamine and bradykinin, which stimulate nerve endings, and the loss of function has a variety of causes which are dependent on the injury.

The acute inflammation process is really quite fascinating. It is initiated by immune cells – such as dendritic cells, macrophages, and mast cells - which are always present in the body. The immune cells from the injured area have components called receptors which allow them to recognize and identify molecules that are produced either as a result of damage or some kind of pathogen. Because these immune cells can recognize these molecules, they are able to initiate the inflammation process.

When some kind of injury occurs, the immune cells become activated and release molecules that start the inflammation process. Vasodilation in the injured area leads to an increase in blood flow and heat (redness). The blood vessels in the area react by leaking plasma proteins and fluid into the tissue to repair injury, which shows up as the physical symptom of swelling. Some of the molecules that are released happen to have a side effect of increasing sensitivity to pain, which likely helps to cause further injury by making us aware that there is a problem and avoiding exacerbating the issue.

Keep in mind, however, that these symptoms are only relevant if the particular inflamed or swollen body part is either on the skin or near it. If not, only some of the PRISH symptoms may be detected.

One good example is an internal organ that doesn't have any nerve endings – such as the lungs – where it's virtually impossible to feel pain, as in the case of certain pneumonias. A person suffering from pneumonia will only start to feel pain when the inflammation starts to push in the inner wall of the chest.

Acute inflammation only lasts as long as the injury-causing material or item is still present in the body; once the initial inflammation process has done its work the acute inflammation stage is over, because the molecules that initiate the process are short-lived and will only be activated as long as the stimulus is present. Once that stage is complete, the body either is healed or moves to chronic inflammation if applicable circumstances are present.

Now let's talk about chronic inflammation. The word chronic implies that this type of inflammation is one that is persistent, happens regularly or lasts for quite a long time, i.e., months. In some cases, chronic inflammation even persists for years on end. For this reason, it is also often referred to as persistent, low-grade inflammation.

What causes chronic inflammation? Among others, it's caused by prolonged exposure to a toxic agent, a persistent injury or infection, or some kind of autoimmune disease. Examples include the body's immune system mistakenly attacking its own healthy tissues (autoimmune disorder), chronic active hepatitis and persistently irritating but low intensity chronic sinusitis, asthma and tuberculosis. Environmental or habitual factors, such as a poor diet, excess weight, stress, lack of exercise, smoking, and excessive alcohol consumption can also cause chronic inflammation. And while inflammation is needed for our bodies' healing processes, too much of a good thing can also be bad. In this case, too much inflammation (chronic) may lead to other, more serious health issues.

Generally speaking, chronic inflammation occurs either when the body believes that there is a threat that requires an inflammatory response, but there in fact is not, or when the threat is real but the inflammatory response is not detected for whatever reason. Unfortunately it is often difficult for chronic inflammation to be detected, although there are tests that are available to diagnose it – the issue is that those tests will only be done if there is some reason to suspect that there is a problem.

# CHAPTER 2: CHRONIC INFLAMMATION AND HEALTH

Health issues like rheumatoid arthritis, asthma, Crohn's disease, ulcerative colitis and lupus – and even strokes, clogged arteries, cancers and heart diseases – can be caused by persistently dilated blood vessels and jacked-up immune systems. And guess what, those blood vessel and immune system conditions are also caused by chronic inflammation.

There is a wide variety of health issues that can be caused or exacerbated by chronic inflammation. This chapter will discuss several of those health concerns, and how chronic inflammation plays a party. If you or a loved one suffer from any of these health issues, this will help you to understand the role that chronic inflammation may play, and how an anti-inflammatory diet can help to manage and regulate those health conditions.

## Atherosclerosis

Atherosclerosis is when the walls of the coronary artery are thickened as a result of plaque and white blood cells accumulating in the blood vessels, usually due to overly high levels of LDL (low-density lipoprotein) molecules. Chronic inflammation is involved because a chronic inflammatory response occurs as a result of the gathering of the white blood cells. Once the chronic inflammatory response kicks in, your body is essentially constantly working to fight off an 'infection' that is not really there. This causes a variety of complications, including angina, myocardial infarction, and stroke.

The role is inflammation in atherosclerosis has only been somewhat recently discovered, and that knowledge may be helpful for detection and treatment of the condition. Certain markers produced by your body during the inflammation process could be detected as a means of diagnosing whether there is a risk or the start of atherosclerosis. In terms of treatment, a method that shuts off, or at least reduces, the inflammatory response may help to decrease the atherosclerosis symptoms.

## Allergies

Allergies are the result of your body having an inappropriate immune response, which leads to inflammation. If you have ever experienced an allergic reaction that involved the area swelling, feeling hot, or turning red, then that was an inflammatory response. The trigger for the reaction is likely not something that is actually a threat to your body, but for whatever reason your immune system has determined that a threat exists and an inflammatory response is required.

Because the allergic reaction in the body involves the releasing of histamine, anti-histamine medications will usually help to resolve the problem. Unfortunately, that is a short-term solution; usually the body's tendency to react to the trigger will continue, leading to repeated allergic responses.

## Myopathies

A myopathy is a muscle disease, where the muscle fibers fail to function for a number of reasons. This leads to reduced muscle strength and function. Inflammatory myopathies occur as a result of the immune system carrying out inappropriate attacks on various muscle components. Pain, swelling, and loss of function can all combine to lead to the reduced function and strength. Inflammatory myopathies can occur in combination with other immune disorders like systemic sclerosis.

## Cancer

While inflammation can help to fight cancer, and certainly does not cause cancer in the first place, it can play a significant role in the spreading of cancerous cells if the right (or rather, wrong) conditions are present. The inflammatory process activates the microenvironment around cancerous tumors, and while the intent of the body is to fight off the intruder, the cancer cells are sometimes able to feed on certain molecules produced during the inflammatory response. This can contribute to the proliferation, survival, and migration of cancer cells.

## HIV and AIDS

While HIV and AIDS are caused by a retro-virus, chronic inflammation plays a substantial role in that virus' ability to impact the body. The inflammation caused by the virus significantly reduced the immune function of the body, permitting the virus to more easily break down the body's systems and functions. In fact, HIV is now thought of as a chronic inflammatory disease as well as a virus-induced immunodeficiency. Recent studies have examined the impact of reducing the inflammation response in order to slow down or stop the progression of HIV and AIDS in the body.

## Diabetes

During the inflammatory process, proteins called cytokines are produced. While they are hugely helpful during an appropriate inflammatory response, they can also get in the way of proper insulin signaling in the body. This can lead to increased insulin resistance and a spike in blood sugar, which in turn can cause white blood cells to attack the 'injured' area. This causes the inflammatory process to continue, essentially developing into a vicious cycle.

## Lung Issues

There many lung conditions and diseases in which chronic inflammation plays a role; these include chronic obstructive pulmonary disease (COPD), asthma, bronchitis, and emphysema. When the lungs become inflamed fluid accumulates, making breathing even more difficult.

## Bone Health

As with diabetes, if for some reason cytokines remain in the body because the acute inflammation process did not resolve itself properly, then the cytokines that continue to be produced will start to interfere with the process of bone remodeling, where old and damaged pieces of bones are replaced with new, strong pieces. If this condition persists, the body will have consistent difficulty in replacing damaged and old bones, leading to loss of bone strength and function.

## Depression

Recent medical studies have discovered that people who struggle with depression have 30 percent more inflammation in the brain than do people who are not depressed. The exact role that chronic inflammation plays in depression and mental health is not yet known, but it is clear that inflammation is involved to some degree.

But the good news is chronic inflammation isn't necessarily being sentenced to death row. Truth is, we can win over chronic inflammation by making certain changes in our lifestyles such as:

-Healthy Eating: A healthy diet is one of the keys to winning against chronic inflammation. It's because chronic inflammation is most often triggered by certain types of foods. When we limit or avoid eating such kinds of inflammation-triggering foods and eating more of non-triggering ones, victory against chronic inflammation is very much within reach.

-Alcohol Consumption: While it's true that consuming "small" amounts of liquor is often linked to lower heart diseases and Alzheimer's risks, excessive drinking of the stuff brings more bacteria easily through the lining of our intestines, leading to inflammation and irritation. The thing however, is that the word "excessive" is quite relative. One thing's for sure though – excessive doesn't necessarily mean drunk. In fact, "healthy" amounts aren't based on whether or not a person gets drunk.

-Smoking: Non-smokers have it better – at least in terms of chronic inflammation – simply because smoking turns on the body's immune system response that causes inflammatory symptoms to activate. It goes without saying then that for winning against chronic inflammation, smoking has to go.

WHILE AN ANTI-INFLAMMATORY DIET WILL NOT NECESSARILY RESOLVE THE UNDERLYING MEDICAL CAUSES OF VARIOUS CONDITIONS AND DISORDERS, IT IS CLEAR THAT INFLAMMATION CAN INCREASE OR EXACERBATE A VARIETY OF MEDICAL ISSUES. AN ANTI-INFLAMMATORY DIET THAT FOCUSES ON REDUCING THE INFLAMMATION IN THE BODY CAN HELP TO AT LEAST REDUCE OR DECREASE SYMPTOMS, EVEN IF THE OVERALL CONDITION WILL NOT BE 'CURED'.

# CHAPTER 3: THE ANTI-INFLAMMATORY DIET

While the term Anti-Inflammatory Diet involves the word "diet", it is not a diet. Well, at least not in the pop culture sense, i.e., a highly restrictive, calorie reduction starvation program. The true definition of diet is "a nutrition or eating program". Simply put, the word diet refers to how we actually eat, which includes the kinds of food we eat, the amounts of such, the frequency at which we consume them and even the timing. Essentially, a diet is all about eating the right foods and avoiding the bad ones for optimal health and fitness. And when we talk about the "right" foods in the anti-inflammatory diet, it means those that minimize or avoid triggering inflammatory symptoms and by "wrong" ones, those that trigger such symptoms. And being a diet, weight loss, slower aging and much better health comes as a bonus for many people who applied the diet in their lives.

A big chunk of this diet is about avoiding or minimizing consumption of particular types of foods that directly trigger or increase the possibility of triggering inflammatory symptoms or responses. Such types of food include sugar and wheat-flour based foods (such as bread and chips), processed foods, fast foods, oils that don't begin with the words coconut/canola/olive and bad fatty food like margarines, pork and beef as well as alcohol and animal proteins (save for yogurt, natural cheeses and fish).

Here's one of the biggest secrets to successfully stay on a diet: variety. Monotony is probably the single biggest reason for most people falling away from healthy diets and adding variety to your food reduces the risk of falling away from the Anti-Inflammatory Diet, assuming you decide to get in on it. That's why eating a wide variety of healthy foods that are high in phytonutrients and fiber (veggies and fruits), starchy fibrous carbohydrates like sweet potatoes, beans, whole grains like bulgur wheat and brown rice, clean proteins from fish and beans, and fatty fishes like salmon and tuna.

Having a collection of recipes that you can use to prepare meals that will fit within the dietary requirements also helps to stick with a nutritional program. This book provides an extensive listing of recipes for dishes that you can prepare that will meet the dietary requirements of the anti-inflammatory diet, and that will also be delicious and healthy for you and for your family.

There are many different factors to consider if you want to make sure that you are eating a properly balanced and nutritious diet. These factors are not specific to the Anti-Inflammatory Diet, but rather are applicable generally to any nutritional plan where you are attempting to lose or maintain weight (for health purposes) and ensure that you are taking in the required amounts of various vitamins and other nutrients.

Try to eat fresh food whenever possible, because in addition to tasting better the fresh versions of foods will usually have higher levels of the nutrients that those foods contain. Frozen foods are a good alternative in a pinch, but fresh foods are always better if possible.

While the Anti-Inflammatory Diet does not focus on weight maintenance or weight loss, the reality is that being at a healthy weight will be much easier on your body than being overweight. If you are already at a healthy weight, then you should make sure that your daily caloric intake is at a level that will maintain that weight; if you are overweight, look at reducing your caloric intake so that you are burning more calories in a day than you are taking in.

For most adults, they will consume between 2,000 and 3,000 calories per day to maintain a healthy weight. Women generally need fewer calories than men, as do smaller people and people who are less active. If you are trying to lose weight, the general idea is that you will lose one pound for every 3500 calories burned, which means that burning 500 calories per day should lead to weight loss of one pound per week.

If you are reducing your caloric intake, always make sure that you do not go below the minimum required level to maintain your bodily functions. For women this minimum is 1,200 calories per day; for men, it is 1,800 calories per day. While a day or two here or there may not have too much of an effect, if you consistently and repeatedly eat less than that required minimum of calories you could experience significant physiological responses as a result of the stress that you have placed on your body by not giving it enough fuel to carry out your essential bodily functions.

Aside from the amount of calories that you are ingesting, in order to make sure that you have a properly balanced diet you should also be aware of how those calories are portioned between carbohydrates, fat, and protein. Ideally, on a daily basis you should be getting 40 to 50 percent of your calories from carbohydrates, 30 percent of the calories from fat, and 20 to 30 percent from protein. You should try to include each of carbohydrates, fat, and protein at each meal. You do not necessarily need to worry about the percentages of carbohydrates, fat, and protein at each meal, as long as your daily totals work in with those recommended percentages.

In terms of carbohydrates, you should try as much as possible to get your carbohydrates from less-refined and less-processed foods that have a low glycemic index. Whole grains and vegetables are preferred over starchy and processed breads and pastas.

For the fat in your diet, you should be aware not only of how much you are eating, but also the kinds of fats that you are eating. Saturated fats should be as low as possible, with polyunsaturated next and monounsaturated in the largest amounts. You can reduce your saturated fat intake by eating less fatty meats and dairy products. Red meat should be avoided as much as possible, not only because it is high in saturated fat but also because it can in some cases contribute to inflammation. Also avoid partially hydrogenated oils, such as those found in margarines and vegetable shortenings. To make sure that you are eating healthy fats whenever possible, include avocados, nuts, salmon and other fish, and eggs rather than red meat.

When it comes to protein, try to focus on protein sources such as beans, lentils, legumes, fish, and poultry, in order to avoid the saturated fats as discussed above. Dairy products can be consumed in moderation, but try to use natural and/or low-fat options when possible. Many dairy products have alternatives made from almonds, rice, oat, soy, or coconut, which are often much lower in fat than their dairy alternatives. If you have liver or kidney problems, or an autoimmune disease, you may need to eat a lower amount of protein; check with your doctor to confirm.

While fiber is not one of the three main components of calories (i.e. fat, carbohydrates, and protein), it is still an important part of your diet. Fiber helps to maintain your digestive system, and increasing your fiber intake will naturally increase the healthiness of your diet because the foods that are highest in fibers tend to be whole grains, vegetables, and fruits.

Phytonutrients are a useful compound found in many foods, which help with fighting inflammation as well as protecting against or treating a variety of other conditions, including cardiovascular disease, neurodegenerative disease, and cancer. In order to make sure that you are getting the most protection possible and eating plenty of phytonutrients, make sure to eat fruits and vegetables that cover the color spectrum, because each color of food will provide different phytonutrients. Look particularly at berries, orange and yellow fruits, tomatoes, and dark leafy greens. Also look at adding soy products to your diet, as they are a good source of phytonutrients and make an excellent protein alternative to meats.

You will also want to make sure that your body is getting all of the vitamins and minerals that it requires. Ensuring that your diet is full of fresh foods, with a lot of fruits, vegetables, whole grains, and legumes, should accomplish this, but you may also want to consult with your doctor to see if you are low on anything and if you need supplements.

You have probably heard more times than you can count that you should drink plenty of water, but it really does provide a vast array of health benefits. Water helps to remove toxins from your body, and provides hydration which is important considering that water plays an important role in virtually every system within your body.

Make sure to snack throughout the day. This does not mean unhealthy snacks like cookies and chips, but rather eating healthy items. The advantage to snacks is that it means that you will be less hungry at the main mealtimes, so you will be more likely to focus on preparing healthy meals that fit with the Anti-Inflammatory Diet rather than eating whatever is available because you have not eaten in too long and do not want to wait. In fact, you may want to consider eating several small meals throughout the day rather than three main meals; in addition to spreading out the calories, it also gives you a bit more variety throughout the day.

These are general rules that apply to a basic healthy diet, whether you are focusing on anti-inflammation or not. There are some rules that you should follow specifically for the Anti-Inflammation Diet as well.

For the purposes of the Anti-Inflammatory Diet, it is recommended that you try to eat at least 25 grams of fiber each day. This will inherently mean that you are eating foods with anti-inflammatory properties, because the foods that are high in fibers also tend to contain the various anti-inflammatory substances.

You should also try and eat a minimum of nine servings of vegetables and fruit each day. One serving means half of a cup of a cooked fruit or vegetable, or one cup of a raw fruit or vegetable.

Each week, you should make sure to ingest four servings each of alliums and crucifers. Alliums include scallions, garlic, leek, and onions, while crucifers are vegetables like cabbage, broccoli, cauliflower, and Brussels sprouts. These foods have powerful antioxidant properties, so in addition to their anti-inflammatory properties they can also potentially lower your risk of cancer.

We already discussed 'healthy' fats earlier in this chapter, but for the purposes of the Anti-Inflammatory Diet it really is important to eat plenty of Omega-3 fatty acids, because they have strong anti-inflammatory properties.

Next up, we'll take a look at some of the best anti-inflammatory foods to pile up at home to help you successfully get on – and stay on – the Anti-Inflammatory Diet. We will also look at foods that should be avoided, especially those that may actually have inflammation responses in your body. If you follow the tips set out in the chapter and focus on eating the foods listed in the next chapter, you will be well-established in the Anti-Inflammatory Diet and on your way to helping your body to fight against chronic inflammation and the medical conditions that it can cause.

# PART II: WHAT TO EAT

# CHAPTER 4: TOP ANTI-INFLAMMATORY FOOD ITEMS

Another key to successfully staying on the Anti-Inflammatory Diet, as with all others, is preparation. In particular, we'll need to stock up our pantries with a good variety of the right food items so that we avoid burning out of the diet by enjoying various delicious flavors. In general, the anti-inflammatory diet includes foods that are typical of a Mediterranean-style diet, including fish, fresh vegetables and fruits, and healthy fats. Moderate portions of nuts and red wine may also be an option, but red meat should be greatly restricted. Omega-3 fatty acids are a main focus of the anti-inflammatory diet because of their ability to inhibit an enzyme in the body that produces prostaglandins, which activate the inflammation process.

Here then, are some of the best – and tastiest, if I may add – food items we'll need to stock up on at home for deliciously beating the living daylights out of chronic inflammation.

## ALMONDS (AND OTHER NUTS)

While most nuts will provide some level of anti-inflammatory assistance, largely due to the Omega-3 fatty acids that they contain, certain kinds of nuts are better than others for this purpose. Almonds in particular are an excellent source of Omega-3 fatty acids, as are cashews and walnuts. The added benefit of nuts is that they are very versatile: they can be added to meals for flavoring, or eaten in-between meals as a healthy and filling snack.

## APPLE CIDER VINEGAR

Apple cider vinegar helps to improve the digestive tract, including reducing inflammation in that area. As an added bonus, if your digestive system is healthy you can process foods better, which can help with weight loss. Apple cider vinegar can be added to your water to help purify it, or added to smoothies if you are not a fan of the flavor of the vinegar. It can also be used as an ingredient in many meals.

## APRICOTS

Phytochemicals can – in some instances – address inflammation. Apricots contain a phytochemical called quercetin which helps to reduce inflammation. Being loaded with the stuff, as well as being a good salad ingredient, apricots make for good additions to our pantry list. Try a spinach salad with almonds and apricots, drizzled with an oil and vinegar dressing, for a delicious, healthy, and anti-inflammatory lunch.

## ASPARAGUS

It's known to be anti-inflammatory and makes for a good ingredient to other dishes or a side dish. 'Nuff said. If that was not enough to encourage you to add asparagus to your diet, it is also considered a 'superfood' because of the wide range of nutrients that it contains. It is best if eaten fresh, but frozen can also work.

## AVOCADO

Really avocado should already be a part of your diet because of the vast variety of nutrients that it provides. In fact, avocadoes are on the list of the healthiest foods on the planet. While avocadoes do have a fair amount of fat, that fat is the 'good' kind: Omega-3 fatty acids, which are exactly what you are looking for in anti-inflammatory foods. Avocado can be added as a side or topping to many meals, and fresh guacamole makes an excellent mid-day snack.

## BASIL (AND OTHER SPICES)

More than just their great flavors, basil and other spices are anti-inflammatory. Again, that's enough reason to be included in our list. It also helps that they are usually included in most recipes already, so you do not have to do much work to incorporate them into your diet.

## BEANS

Anti-inflammatory properties, complex carb and fiber are enough great reasons for these to be in our pantries. Beans are commonly found as a side dish in many restaurants, and they are cheap to purchase from the grocery store and easy to prepare. There are many, many recipes that contain beans, so including them in your diet will be very simple.

## BEETS

A very good indication that a food is full of antioxidants is when it is a deep, rich color, and beets are a perfect example of this. Beets contain the antioxidant betalain, which helps cells to repair damage caused by inflammation. Beets also contain potassium and magnesium, which help to fight inflammation. Magnesium deficiency has been linked quite strongly with inflammatory issues. This is because the body is not good at processing calcium without magnesium, and if calcium is allowed to build up in the body then it starts to be identified by the body as an unwanted foreign object which will trigger the inflammation process.

## BELL PEPPERS

Flavonoids give this food item super anti-oxidant powers that make it one of the best weapons against free-radicals and consequently, inflammation. It's also deliciously low calorie, making it a good addition to our list. Try to incorporate all of the different colors of pepper into your diet, so that you get the whole spectrum of flavonoids. Plus your meals will be much more aesthetically pleasing if you have a variety of colors, which will make you more excited about eating.

## BLUEBERRIES, RASPBERRIES AND BLACKBERRIES

This Holy Trinity of anti-inflammatory nutrition is – pardon the pun – berry rich in phytochemicals and antioxidants, which make them excellent additions to our anti-inflammatory pantry stock list. As mentioned earlier, anti-oxidants take care of free-radicals that trigger inflammation responses. It may also help to think that they taste great in cakes, smoothies and pies.

## BOK CHOY

Related to broccoli and cauliflower, bok choy contains extremely high levels of beta-carotene. The body converts beta-carotene into vitamin A, which helps with the health of skin, eyes, and the immune system. While bok choy may not be a standard vegetable in North American diets, it is easy to make and can be added to any recipe that includes a mix of vegetables, such as soups or stir-fries.

## BROCCOLI

This super food really doesn't need introductions because it's one of the most popular healthy foods around. It contains some protein, lots of fiber, loaded with Vitamin C and – wait for it – anti-inflammatory. It's also deliciously flexible, which means that it can be cooked in a myriad number of ways, and can also be bought fresh or frozen.

## BRUSSELS SPROUTS

While these may leave you with some negative memories from your childhood, the reality is that Brussels sprouts should be on the list for every diet or nutritional program due to their incredible nutritional value. Like avocadoes, Brussels sprouts are on the list of the healthiest foods on the planet thanks to the plethora of health benefits that they provide. They have anti-inflammatory properties, are an excellent source of protein to help your digestive system, and also provide protein. And there are many other ways to eat Brussels sprouts other than the traditional (and perhaps less appetizing) steaming.

## BUCKWHEAT

Buckwheat has not yet made its mark in North American diets, although it is hugely popular in Japan and other areas of Asia. Buckwheat is often eaten in noodle form, although it is available in other forms as well. Buckwheat noodles make an excellent alternative to starchier noodles and also provide anti-inflammatory benefits.

## CABBAGE

Its anthocyanin content is what makes it one of nature's most potent anti-inflammatory foods around. It's also deliciously versatile being made into soups, coleslaw, sautéed veggie treat or as an ingredient in other deliciously healthy dishes. Red cabbage is the best choice as it has the highest level of anthocyanins, but any variety will provide some anti-inflammatory benefits.

## CANTALOUPE

Aside from tasting great and making a yummy snack or dessert, cantaloupe also contains phytonutrients which have anti-inflammatory properties. Cantaloupes are also a good source of antioxidants, and have very high levels of vitamins A and C. Just remember that it also contains a fair amount of sugar (even if it is natural sugar), so you will want to restrict your portions – think of cantaloupe as a treat rather than a daily food.

## CARROTS

More than just being anti-inflammatory, it's also full of Vitamin A and beta-carotene – both of which make for excellent anti-inflammatory nutrients. While it's very flexible in that it can be used to prepare many delicious dishes, the best way to fully utilize its nutritious anti-inflammatory properties is by eating it raw or by juicing it using a food processing or NutriBullet machine to enjoy deliciously healthy smoothies.

## CAULIFLOWER

Loaded with tons of Vitamins C and K, which by the way are 2 of nature's most powerful anti-oxidants, cauliflower is one deliciously wonderful cruciferous anti-inflammatory veggie that's worth stocking up our pantries with. You can enjoy it as the main dish or be grated finely into a very good rice substitute for enjoying different delicious meals with.

## CELERY

Celery is a food that is discussed in the context of most diets or nutritional plans, thanks to its extremely low calorie content and high fiber content. If you do not like to eat it raw, you can throw it into a blender with other vegetables for a smoothie. It also makes an excellent soup base, along with onions and garlic.

## CHIA SEEDS

Chia seeds are another food item that contain high levels of Omega-3 fatty acids and Omega-6 fatty acids, which are best for your body when eaten in balance with each other. As a result of their Omega-3 fatty acid levels, chia seeds provide extensive antioxidant and anti-inflammatory properties, which actually allows them to help to reverse inflammation, as well as lowering blood pressure and regulating cholesterol. Needless to say, chia seeds are one food item that absolutely should be added to your diet if you are following the Anti-Inflammatory Diet.

## CHICKEN

For the anti-inflammatory diet, we are talking about organic chicken and not those hormones-loaded commercial variants that can be easily bought in most grocery stores. While chicken in and by itself isn't anti-inflammatory, it is a good source of clean protein, which is one of the things we may miss out on the Anti-Inflammatory Diet given we'll be ditching all meat products. And we need protein to maintain good muscle mass and for feeling fuller for longer (satiety).

## CINNAMON

While we did discuss spices in general above, cinnamon deserves its own mention. Cinnamon has been used for centuries as a natural treatment for a wide variety of health conditions. It has both antioxidant and anti-inflammatory properties, and is a lovely addition to many different dishes. Sprinkle in a little cinnamon to soups, salads, and desserts to help your body fight inflammation.

## CUCUMBER

More than just being anti-inflammatory, cucumber is alkaline-forming and rich in anti-oxidants. It's also deliciously versatile.

## CURRY POWDER

As with cinnamon, curry powder has enough anti-inflammatory properties that it deserves to be mentioned outside of the general 'spices' category. Studies have shown that in cultures where curry spices are a staple in the traditional diet, those cultures tend to have lower incidences of inflammation-based medical conditions. Curry can be a welcome addition to soups in particular.

## DARK CHOCOLATE

If you were thinking that you would need to abandon all sweets in order to follow the Anti-Inflammatory Diet, think again! While you will need to limit the amount of chocolate that you eat, dark chocolate does actually have mild anti-inflammatory properties. It does have to be dark chocolate, though; milk chocolate actually adds to inflammation because of its dairy content, and its high levels of sugar do not help either.

## EGGS

Just like oats, an egg called by any other name wouldn't be as anti-inflammatory. That's because all eggs aren't like humans that are supposedly created equal. In particular, cage-free or free-range eggs are far more superior to those that were from chickens raised in cages in terms of being anti-inflammatory. They may cost more but they're worth the premium.

Eggs can be especially helpful in our Anti-Inflammatory Diet, considering that we'll need to cut down on a lot of meat products and hence, get less protein. Consuming free-range or cage-free eggs can go a long way towards helping us meat our daily protein requirements.

Eggs are also very satiating, which reduces our risks for binge-eating and eating garbage foods. As such, it can also help feel more satisfied and stay on the diet.

## EXTRA VIRGIN OLIVE OIL

This isn't just a versatile oil, it's also a super one! More than just making foods taste great, extra-virgin olive oil contains so much anti-inflammatory properties. This makes it another indispensable food item in our pantries.

## FENNEL

While fennel has been known as a source of many important nutrients for some time, as we learn more about it we continue to discover additional health benefits. Fennel contains high levels of phytonutrients, which provide anti-inflammatory benefits, and also contains antioxidants. If you are not familiar with fennel, do a quick internet search – there are many recipes that include fennel as an ingredient and that will fit within the Anti-Inflammatory Diet.

## FLAXSEED

Flaxseed contains lignans and alpha-Linolenic acids, both of which have anti-inflammatory properties. Flaxseed is very easy to add to dishes: sprinkle it in soups or salads, or add it to smoothies.

## GARLIC

If our pantry food stocks list were like boxing, garlic would probably be (sadly) Floyd Mayweather – the undisputed champion and pound-for-pound the best in our stock list. It's that good that supplements are created out of its extracts. More than just its anti-inflammatory powers, garlic is one important ingredient in many delicious recipes. So regardless if we're on the Anti-Inflammatory Diet or not, garlic should be one of those indispensable food items in our pantries.

## GINGER

I don't know if it's just a coincidence but gingers are chock full of – surprise – gingerols! In case you're wondering, it's what gives ginger its anti-inflammatory properties. It's also filled with antioxidants, which we already know to be very good nutrients for combatting chronic inflammation. It's deliciously versatile too as it can be used in preparing many delicious dishes, as a condiment (Hainanese chicken, anyone?) and even as a tea.

## GOJI BERRIES

Goji berries – also known as wolfberries – are native to China and other regions of Asia, and have been used as a medicinal plant there for centuries. Goji berries are another super food: they are a good source of many vitamins and minerals, including vitamins A and C, fiber, iron, zinc, and antioxidants, and they also contain all 8 essential amino acids that are needed from diet. And for the purposes of the Anti-Inflammatory Diet, goji berries do also have anti-inflammatory properties.

Keep in mind that you should consult with a medical professional before introducing goji berries into your diet on any kind of regular basis, because they can interact with certain medications, and they have unexpectedly high levels of certain vitamins and nutrients which can actually lead to toxicity if you eat too much.

GRAPEFRUIT

Both pink and red grapefruit contain anti-inflammatory components, as well as antioxidants. The fact that they are relatively low in sugar content makes them a great addition to your diet. Grapefruit juice can be drunk on its own or added to smoothies, and grapefruit makes a refreshing and delicious breakfast or mid-morning snack.

GREEN TEA (AND OTHER TEAS)

As we've been harping since time immemorial, anti-oxidants are very effective in combatting free radicals, which can trigger inflammation responses in our bodies. Green teas are chock full of anti-oxidants and flavonoids, two of the best anti-inflammatory agents on earth, which easily makes it one of our Anti-Inflammatory Diet pantry staples.

And more than just the anti-inflammatory benefits, they're also very good sources of steady and slow acting caffeine, which helps us keep awake and alert better than coffee and energy drinks. Coffees and energy drinks can give us caffeine crashes that are similar in effect to sugar crashes and hence, inferior caffeine sources than tea.

## HOT SAUCE

While your automatic reaction to hot sauce might be to assume that it would cause inflammation, thanks to the heat and spiciness, it actually can have an anti-inflammatory effect thanks to the capsaicin that most hot sauces contain. However, if heartburn is one of the inflammatory issues that you are trying to deal with through this diet, you will likely want to avoid hot sauce.

## KALE

Like bok choy and spinach, kale is an incredibly nutrient-dense food. Kale has very high levels of vitamins A and C, antioxidants, and anti-inflammatory properties. In fact, some medical professionals believe that kale has such anti-inflammatory benefits that it may actually help to reverse certain inflammatory conditions. Kale makes a great addition to smoothies, soups, and salads.

## KELP

As with some of the other foods on this list, kelp is not necessarily a common part of the North American diet, but that does not mean that it should not be. Kelp is a great source of iodine and fiber, and its high levels of fucoidan provide an anti-inflammatory effect. It may be difficult to find fresh kelp in the grocery store, but supplements are easily found.

## KIWI

Kiwi provides a lower level of anti-inflammatory benefits than many of the foods on this list, but it does provide it to some degree, and it is a nice sweet food to be able to add into your diet on occasion as a treat. You can have it as part of your breakfast, as a snack, or add it to your smoothies for extra flavor.

## LEMONS AND LIMES

These two seemingly siblings are rich in anti-oxidants, which help fight free radicals. More than just causing cancer, free radicals can also cause inflammation. As such, these two sour siblings make it to our anti-inflammatory pantry hall of fame.

Oh, more than just loaded with anti-oxidant, they're also alkaline, which is very good for our health.

## LENTILS

Lentils are one discontent bunch. They're not comfortable with just being anti-inflammatory – they also want to be complete meals! In fact, they are with their high protein, fiber and complex carbohydrate contents. They're very easy to prepare in many different and delicious ways (do I read flexibility?) and work together with many other food items either as the leader or supporter for an even greater variety of delicious dishes.

## MANGOSTEEN

Mangosteen is a fruit that grows in South East Asia and some areas of Africa, and has been used by cultures there for centuries as a source of medicines. Although sweet, the fruit is actually quite low in calories, contains no fat, and is very rich in dietary fiber. As if that were not enough, it is also an excellent source of antioxidants and vitamin C, and has anti-inflammatory properties. It is used in the treatment of many different medical conditions, including Alzheimer's disease, cancer, high blood pressure, and of course immune disorders.

Mangosteen fruit can be harmful to fetuses, so pregnant women should avoid ingesting it. Other than that, it has no known negative health effects.

## OATS

It's important to know that unlike roses, an oat by any other name is no longer the same, anti-inflammatory oat. When it comes to the battling chronic inflammation, our best bet is the steel-cut variant and not those instant types, especially those that come in sugar and artificial ingredients-laden flavors.

Other good bonuses that come with eating steel-cut oats is that they're a great source of sustainable energy and makes us feel fuller for longer, reducing the risk for binge-eating and eating really bad food.

## ONIONS

Onions contain a lot of the ingredient quercetin, which gives it some level of anti-inflammatory property. And more than just the anti-inflammatory benefit, it's also very versatile and cheap! As such, our pantries shouldn't run out of this versatile and deliciously cheap super food.

## ORANGES

Deliciously flexible and chock full of phytonutrients and anti-inflammatory benefits – what more can we ask for? In particular, it's loaded with antioxidants and flavonoids, and high levels of vitamin C. We must ensure our pantries never go out of stock with oranges. There are some people who will have difficulty eating citrus foods, and it can exacerbate certain conditions such as heartburn. But if citrus is not a concern for you, then you should definitely consider incorporating oranges into your diet on a more regular basis.

## OYSTERS AND SHRIMPS

Oh, these deliciously marvelous seafood items must be in our diets, unless we're allergic to them, of course. For one, shrimps contain generous servings of astaxanthin, which is a good anti-inflammatory agent. Oysters are also believed to be anti-inflammatory (even if just mildly) and not just for making people horny (aphrodisiac).

One thing we'll need to keep in mind when eating these items is that they have relatively high levels of cholesterol than most other food items. As such, we'll need to keep close tabs on our consumption of the stuff. It'll be good to eat a bit more veggies and fruits with these.

## PAPAYA

One of the reasons it makes our anti-inflammatory pantry stocks list is that it contains nutrients that aren't usually found in other fruits and veggies, which makes it one of the best anti-inflammatory food items around. It's also versatile as it can be eaten alone or as part of delicious salads and exotic dishes like the Filipino chicken dish called Tinola.

## PINEAPPLE

Pineapples are one of those super foods that aren't just rich in nutrients but also deliciously versatile – can be enjoyed fresh, canned, frozen and pureed. However, we should limit our consumption of this super food, particularly if our blood sugar levels are already high to begin with.

## PUMPKIN

Apart from being a good anti-inflammatory food item, pumpkin's one of the most flexible veggies on the face of God's green earth. As such, it's definitely one food item to keep in the pantry. Just how versatile this is? We can make desserts out of it (pumpkin pie), soups and even roasts. And remember, versatility's the name of the game here in order to successfully stay on the Anti-Inflammatory Diet.

## QUINOA

If you haven't started eating this super food just yet, I suggest you do so now. Why? For one, it's one of the few food items in the world that contain good amounts of both protein and fiber! Add to that its vitamin and mineral content for excellent total body nutrition and you have one heckuva super food in your hands – and mouth.

But of course, the real reason why it's on our list is it being one of the best anti-inflammatory food items around. And here's an added bonus: delicious variety! You can use quinoa in many delicious recipes and as such, it should be part of our pantries' stockpiles.

## RED WINE

Just like sweets, you do not have to give up all alcohol to follow the Anti-Inflammatory Diet. While most alcohols should be avoided, red wine has such high levels of antioxidants and flavanoids that it actually has anti-inflammatory benefits. Red wine should be consumed in moderation, but a glass or two is acceptable.

## SALMON

One of the best fishes to enjoy for battling chronic inflammation is salmon. It's because salmon is chock full of Omega 3 fatty acids, a nutrient that's scientifically proven to be very beneficial for chronic inflammation. It's also a very good way to bring balance to excessive consumption of another fatty acid – Omega 6.

## SHIITAKE MUSHROOMS

These mushrooms in particular make a great addition to the Anti-Inflammatory Diet, because they contain an anti-inflammatory substance called polysaccharides. You can substitute shiitake mushrooms for virtually any other kind of mushroom in your recipes, and are easily found in grocery stores, so there should not be a problem with adding these mushrooms into your diet.

## SPINACH

Well, this super food isn't just for a particularly famous sailor with an out-of-this-world set of forearms attached to a pair of really tiny upper arms. Apart from being one of the best anti-inflammatory foods around, spinach is chock full of protein, fiber and phytonutrients. It's also known to help minimize risks for cancers and heart diseases.

And remember the versatility game? It's one good player to have on our team because there's a ton of recipes we can use to prepare it. From smoothies to salads, the possibilities are (relatively) endless! And that's why it should be part of our regular anti-inflammatory pantry stockpile items.

## SWEET POTATOES

If you're a big potato junkie but would like to experience more anti-inflammatory benefits and eat more fiber, sweet potatoes are just what the doctor ordered. Just avoid deep-frying them if you'd like to keep it anti-inflammatory and simply bake or boil them. Some restaurants will offer baked sweet potato as an alternative to a regular baked potato. It is also easy to make mashed sweet potatoes instead of the standard mashed potatoes.

## SWISS CHARD

Similar to kale and spinach, swiss chard is high in antioxidants and anti-inflammatories, but it has a unique flavor so will add variety to your diet. It is quite versatile, and can be used in salads, soups, stir fries, smoothies, and other dishes.

## TOMATOES

Tomatoes are so anti-inflammatory and versatile that it makes it to our anti-inflammatory pantry stockpile hall of fame! More than just the anti-inflammatory benefits, it's also full of beneficial nutrients, particularly lycopene that's very, very good for heart health. And speaking of versatility, we can also eat them as they are – cooked or raw – or as part of other recipes as sauces and toppings.

TURKEY

Like chicken, turkey does not have particularly high anti-inflammatory properties, but it does not contribute to inflammation like red meats do so it makes a great alternative to red meats and other high-fat proteins. Also as with chicken, try to purchase organic varieties when you can, and also avoid pre-prepared cold cuts which are very high in negative additives and nitrates.

TURMERIC

This is another spice that deserves its own mention for its anti-inflammatory benefits. Turmeric contains a substance called curcumin, which is also found in curry, and this is what gives turmeric its anti-inflammatory properties. Turmeric also can help with weight loss, and may even play a role in fighting cancer. Try to find recipes that will use this spice and otherwise fit within the Anti-Inflammatory Diet so that you can get the health benefits of this super-spice.

TURNIPS

Turnips have relatively high levels of Omega-3 fatty acids and vitamin K, which makes them a great option for the Anti-Inflammatory Diet. Very few vegetables have high levels of Omega-3's, which makes turnips fairly unique in the vegetable category. Raw turnip can be added to salads, you can roast or bake them, or you can add them to smoothies. If you are cooking turnip make sure to follow the recipe carefully, because it is easy to undercook or overcook them.

## WATERMELON

Watermelon contains a substance called lycopene, which is a cellular inhibitor that plays a role in certain inflammatory processes and also works as an antioxidant. Watermelon also contains a substance called choline, which helps to reduce chronic inflammation. In addition to these excellent properties, it also happens to be delicious and very refreshing, so it would make a fantastic addition to your Anti-Inflammatory Diet. Watermelon can be eaten on its own, or included in salads or smoothies.

## ZUCCHINI

While not quite as high in anti-inflammatory properties as kale or spinach, zucchini still has good levels of anti-inflammatory properties and also is a great source of many other nutrients. Easy to prepare and versatile, zucchini makes a great addition to the Anti-Inflammatory Diet.

## SUPPLEMENTATION

While the best way to get important nutrients for managing chronic inflammation is through whole, natural foods, it can be very hard for many people to get enough by simply eating. One reason is declining nutrient density of crops due to soil fatigue and non-stop farming. As such, we may need to take food supplements in order to get enough anti-inflammatory nutrients. Here are some of the best anti-inflammatory supplements we can take.

### *Vitamin A*

Commonly found in liver, whole milk and several fortified food items, Vitamin A is an anti-oxidant, which helps fight free-radicals that contribute to inflammatory symptoms on top of causing cancers and other diseases. Vitamin A deficiency has been linked to higher risks for inflammation in the skin, lungs and intestines.

### *Vitamin B6*

This particular vitamin is commonly found in fish, veggies, turkey and beef. However, its water-soluble nature means our bodies consistently flush out this important vitamin and as such, supplementation may be needed to ensure adequate amounts of it in our bodies. Deficiency in this vitamin can lead to increase levels of the inflammatory indicator called C-reactive protein, which is linked to heart disease.

## *Vitamin C*

Vitamin C serves many different purposes in our bodies like collagen production and strengthening the immune system, among others. Found mainly in citrus fruits like oranges, it's one of the most effective antioxidants around, which we know can be quite beneficial in terms of managing free radicals and consequently, inflammation. Studies have shown it can also help lower the inflammatory marker C-reactive protein.

## *Vitamin D*

More than just working together with calcium to give us stronger bones, it's also an anti-inflammatory ally. It's mostly found in egg yolks, beef, liver and fish and can be produced by our bodies when we're exposed to the sun. Vitamin D deficiency has been linked to several inflammatory diseases like rheumatoid arthritis and inflammatory bowel disease, among others.

## Vitamin E

Another excellent antioxidant that can help us manage chronic inflammation together as part of the Anti-Inflammatory Diet. This is commonly found in leafy green veggies, seeds and nuts. While it comes in several forms, researchers suggest that alpha-tocopherol may be most beneficial form of Vitamin E, particularly in terms of slowing down the release of inflammatory substances that can result in heart damage and in terms of easing lung inflammation.

Vitamin E comes in several different forms. Some research suggests the alpha-tocopherol type may help prevent heart disease by slowing the release of inflammatory substances that damage the heart.

## Vitamin K

Abundantly available in green veggies like spinach, kale, broccoli and asparagus, it may be able to help reduce levels of certain inflammation markers in our bodies, studies suggest.

## Aloe

We all know that aloe vera is a great way to treat cuts, scratches, and burns, but it is also very useful as a dietary supplement. The same gel that you apply to your skin, directly from the plant, can be made into pill or tablet form. Do not ever eat the gel directly from the plant; processing is required to make it safe to ingest!

Aloe has various anti-inflammatory benefits, especially for those dealing with arthritis, joint inflammation, and inflammation in muscles, skin, and connective tissue. Aloe has the added benefit of assisting to regulate the digestive track.

## *Astaxanthin*

Astaxanthin is a type of substance known as carotenoid, which is a natural pigment founds in certain plants and bacteria, as well as in salmon, plankton, and krill. The most common source of astaxanthin is algae, which has the largest proportion of the substance at around 40,000 parts per million. It is commonly used as a nutritional supplement for both humans and livestock, and to date there are no known side effects.

In humans, astaxanthin is used primarily as an antioxidant, and is up to 10 times stronger than other carotenoids used for the same purpose. It also has anti-inflammatory purposes, which makes it an excellent supplement for the Anti-Inflammatory Diet.

## *Bromelain*

Found naturally in pineapple, this enzyme works to reduce inflammation by altering the migration and activation of leukocytes (white blood cells), which form part of the inflammatory process. Bromelain is available most commonly in capsule form, and is often taken for digestive issues as well as an anti-inflammatory.

## *Cod Liver Oil*

Although cod liver oil may seem very unappetizing to many people, it does have extensive health benefits. Cod liver oil has been used by peoples in northern Europe for centuries to help with the negative effects of the long, cold, dark winters, and specifically to help with aching joints, rheumatism, and stiff muscles. Traditionally it was obtained by eating the fresh liver of the *Gadus morhua* (cod) fish, but today it is easily accessible as a supplement in a variety of forms.

Cod liver oil is extremely nutrient dense; it is a source of vitamins D and A, and anti-inflammatory Omega-3 fatty acids. In addition to its anti-inflammatory properties, cod liver oil can also help with lowering cholesterol, treating diabetes, preventing heart disease, lowering high blood pressure, treating depression, and protecting from eye disorders. If you do not avoid fish for other dietary reasons, then cod liver oil is a fantastic supplement to help with the Anti-Inflammatory Diet and deal with many other health issues as well.

## Cat's Claw

Cat's claw is a woody vine that is native to Central and South America, and particularly in the Amazon rainforest. It gets its name from its thorns, which resemble a cat's claws. The Incas used Cat's claw for a variety of medicinal purposes, including inflammation and infections. Today it is used to treat even more conditions, including cancer, digestive issues, viral infections, and parasites.

Cat's claw can be obtained in several different forms, including liquid extracts, tablets, capsules, and tea. While there are few known side effects, women who are pregnant or trying to become pregnant should avoid taking Cat's claw because it has historically been used to prevent and abort pregnancy.

## Devil's Claw

This herb, which is native to Africa, is also called 'hook plant' because of its fruit which is covered with hooks. The plant, and particularly its roots and tubers, has been used for many centuries for various medicinal purposes. Devil's claw has anti-inflammatory properties, and is used in particular for dealing with atherosclerosis, arthritis, and allergies, among any other uses.

You should be aware that Devil's claw can impact how the liver breaks down certain medications, so could alter the side effects of those medications. Speak with a medical professional before introducing Devil's claw as a supplement to your diet.

## *Flax Oil (Flaxseed Oil)*

Similar to flaxseed discussed under the anti-inflammatory foods section, flaxseed oil also has anti-inflammatory properties thanks to its high levels of Omega-3 fatty acids. Flax oil (and Omega-3's generally) also help with the digestive and cardiovascular systems, and can also contribute to healthier eyes, skin, hair, and nails.

You can purchase flax oil in soft gel or liquid capsules. Check to see if the capsules that you purchase require refrigeration; many do because flax oil is easily broken down by heat, light, or oxygen.

Flax oil can potentially slow down the rate at which your body absorbs other nutritional supplements or oral medications that you are taking, so you should check with a medical professional before introducing flax oil into your diet as a supplement.

## *Frankincense*

Frankincense is an oil that comes from the resin of the Boswellia carteri trees that grow in Kenya. It has anti-inflammatory properties, and also is commonly used topically to deal with various skin conditions. You can purchase Frankincense as an essential oil, and to digest it you just dilute one drop of the oil in 4 fluid ounces of liquid (e.g. water).

## Maitake Mushrooms

Maitake mushrooms are a kind of mushroom that are native to Japan, and have been used there as a medicinal plant for centuries. They are under the supplement section in this book, however, because they are difficult to find in North America in mushroom form but easy to find in supplement form.

Maitake mushrooms contain a polysaccharide called beta-D-glucan, which helps to stimulate the immune system. It has been studied specifically with respect to fighting cancer, but does have benefits for the overall immune system.

You can purchase maitake in supplement form either as an extract or in powdered capsules.

## Noni

While Noni is actually a fruit that is indigenous to the Pacific tropics, it is rarely consumed in fruit form. It is most commonly ingested as a drink, bottled either in pure form or in combination with other fruit juices. You can also purchase Noni in tea, capsule, and tablet forms. Noni has antioxidant and anti-inflammatory properties, and also helps to regulate the digestive system. Studies are being carried out to see if it might also assist in the fight against cancer.

It is important to note that Noni is quite high in potassium, so anyone on a potassium-restricted diet should consult with a medical professional before taking this as a supplement.

## Resveratrol

This is a substance that is found in several types of plants, including grapes, blueberries, and raspberries, and is produced by the plant in response to injury. This is the substance that gives red wine its anti-inflammatory properties. Resveratrol helps to reduce inflammation by preventing your body from creating two kinds of molecules that are known to activate the inflammation process. It also has antioxidant properties.

## Walnut Oil

In the food section, we looked at nuts as an addition to the Anti-Inflammatory Diet. While many different types of nuts will offer anti-inflammatory benefits, when it comes to oils made from nuts, walnut oil is the best. This is because walnut oil happens to come out of processing maintaining very high levels of the nutrients that are found in the nuts; 35 grams of walnut oil will provide the same nutritional offerings as 50 grams of walnuts.

In addition to its anti-inflammatory properties, which arise from its high levels of Omega-3 fatty acids, walnut oil can also help to lower cholesterol and is a good source of antioxidants.

You can use walnut oil in your cooking, although it is best used in cold dishes because its slightly nutty taste can go bitter when heated. You can also take a daily dose just as a supplement, if you prefer.

## *Willow Bark*

Willow bark has been used for as long as 6,000 years to treat various medical conditions, including pain, inflammation, and musculoskeletal problems. Willow bark contains a chemical called salicin, which works very similarly to aspirin. It helps to ease inflammation and pain by inhibiting the inflammation process.

You can purchase willow bark in several forms, including capsules, tables, liquid, and powder. People with an allergy to aspirin or any condition that recommends avoiding ingesting aspirin should also avoid ingesting willow bark.

## *Zinc*

Zinc is an essential mineral that is available in certain foods, including oysters and poultry, but is also commonly taken as a dietary supplement. Its most common application is to boost the immune system, but it can also help to reduce or prevent inflammation.

Each of the foods and dietary supplements listed above are excellent additions to your diet, which will help you to follow the Anti-Inflammatory Diet and fight against chronic inflammation. You will have noted throughout the chapter that certain items, particularly the supplements, had notes about potential side effects and contra-indications, and a tip to consult with your medical professional before ingesting them. Really, this applies to all of the foods and particularly the supplements discussed in this chapter; it is always best to speak with a medical professional before starting on any significant dietary change or taking oral supplements. But if you speak with the relevant medical professionals and make sure that you are following the applicable guidelines, these foods and supplements will be a huge help to you in your fight against chronic inflammation.

## *Foods To Avoid*

Knowing which foods are good to eat is very helpful, but it is also necessary to know which foods you should avoid. There are certain foods that can actually trigger inflammation responses in your body, and you should try to avoid these whenever possible.

## 1. Trans Fats

Trans fats can cause an inflammation response in the body by damage cells in the lining of the blood vessels. In addition, trans fats are not good for your cholesterol, and can cause other health issues as well. Look for the words 'hydrogenated' or 'partially hydrogenated' on food labels, and leave those foods on the shelf.

## 2. Sugar

This likely is not much of a surprise, given how much information has come out in the last few years about the negative impact that sugar has on our bodies. It is believed that sugar is actually more addictive than cocaine, and the withdrawal symptoms experienced by people who remove sugar from their diet would seem to support this. If the sugar levels in your body are too high, this can cause your body to send out extra cytokines, which activate the inflammation response. Avoid sugar whenever possible, especially when it comes to refined and added sugars; natural sugars found in fruits and vegetables tend to be much less of a problem.

## 3. White Breads and Starchy Pastas

These foods are a problem because they are made up of simple carbohydrates, which are easily broken down by your body into sugar. When you eat these refined and processed food items, your body is flooded with high levels of sugar rather quickly, which as discussed above can lead to the over-production of cytokines that trigger the inflammation response.

## 4. Red Meat

There are a number of studies that have linked the animal fats found in red meat to inflammation. There are many reasons for this. One reason is that saturated fats alter the bacteria in our guts, which can trigger the inflammation response. In addition, saturated fats contain a compound called arachidonic acid, which is used by the body to create inflammation. Studies have shown that diets low in this compound have anti-inflammatory effects and have even been shown to possibly improve the symptoms of people suffering from rheumatoid arthritis.

Certain levels of saturated fats are required, but make sure to eat it in moderation; saturated fats should constitute only about 10 percent of your daily caloric intake.

## 5. Alcohol

One or two drinks here or there should not present too much of a problem, but the concern is that if too much alcohol is consumed this allows bacteria to pass through the intestinal lining more easily. This increase in bacteria in the intestines can lead to irritation and inflammation.

Alcohol is also, like white bread and pastas, simple carbohydrates, which means that your body is provided with high levels of sugar all at once, which can trigger an inflammation response. If you are going to drink alcohol, try and stick to red wine if possible because, as discussed in the 'recommended foods' section, it actually has anti-inflammatory properties.

## 6. Omega-6 Fatty Acids

We have talked a lot in this book about Omega-3 fatty acids and the benefits that they can provide to an anti-inflammatory diet. Omega-6 fatty acids are not necessarily bad in and of themselves; rather in North American diets we tend to naturally get more Omega-6 than Omega-3's, and that imbalance can lead to inflammation.

## 7. Dairy

Like with red meat, dairy contains animal fats that can trigger an inflammation response in your body. A moderate amount of low-fat dairy products can actually help to guard against inflammation, but it must be low-fat and done in moderation; you will still need to avoid whole milk or even two percent. Keep in mind also that a significant portion of North American adults has difficulty digesting dairy to some degree, which could in itself trigger an inflammatory response. Given how easy it is today to find non-dairy alternatives to most dairy products, it should be easy to significantly reduce the amount of dairy that you include in your diet.

## 8. MSG

We have known for some time that MSG can have negative effects on the body – including on cardiovascular disease and high blood pressure – but it turns out that it can also trigger an inflammatory response in your body. The cause of this is not yet clear, but it likely has something to do with the fact that MSG is not a chemical that your body would naturally be prepared to do with, and that may cause your body to treat it as a threatening foreign object.

## 9. Gluten

Even if you do not suffer from celiac disease, in today's society there are many people with gluten sensitivity or intolerance. Many people experience bloating or digestive problems as a result of eating gluten, and this may be caused by your body having an inflammatory response to gluten. If you are not prepared to eliminate gluten from your diet completely, then you should at least try to limit the amount that you eat and choose gluten-free options when available.

Each of the foods listed above are best avoided if you want to reduce your body's inflammation response and potentially prevent inflammation entirely, but the fact is that they are also best avoided for a variety of other health reasons. While eating these foods very occasionally may not cause issues, having them as a result and consistent part of your diet could very well contribute to or even be the primary cause of any chronic inflammation that you may be dealing with. It is best to just avoid these foods and focus on eating the anti-inflammatory foods discussed earlier in this chapter.

# CHAPTER 5: ANTI-INFLAMMATORY DIET RECIPES

Now that we've stocked our pantries with the top anti-inflammatory foods in the market, it's time to learn deliciously anti-inflammatory recipes that will not just help us get on the Anti-Inflammatory Diet but stay on it as well.

## BREAKFAST

### 1. Quinorridge

Ingredients:

- -1 cup water;

- -1 tablespoon honey;

- -1/2 cup dried unsweetened cherries;

- -1/2 cup dry quinoa;

- -1/2 teaspoon vanilla extract; and

- -1/4 teaspoon ground cinnamon.

Instructions:

- -Except for the honey, mix all the ingredients well and bring to a boil on medium-high heat. Reduce the heat as soon as the mixture begins boiling and cover to simmer for 15 minutes or when the quinoa has already absorbed all liquids and becomes tender.

-Drizzle with honey after taking the mixture off the heat to enjoy.

## 2. Gingery Oats

Ingredients:

-1 cup water;

-1 tablespoon flaxseeds;

-1 tablespoon molasses;

-1 teaspoon ground ginger;

-1/2 cup steel-cut oats;

-1/2 teaspoon cinnamon ground;

-1/4 cup unsweetened cherries, dried; and

-1/4 teaspoon nutmeg, ground.

Instructions:

-Except for the flaxseeds and molasses, bring all the other ingredients to a boil over medium-high heat in a saucepan. When the mixture starts to boil, bring the heat down to simmer for about 6 minutes or until the steel-cut oats have absorbed all the liquid.

-After removing from heat, mix the flaxseeds in. After letting the mixture stand for about 5 minutes, drizzle the oats with molasses.

### 3. Eggomatoes

Ingredients:

- -1 teaspoon fresh Italian parsley;

- -2 pieces large eggs;

- -2 pieces large fresh tomatoes;

- -Salt and pepper for tasting;

Instructions:

- -While you're preheating your oven to 350 degrees Fahrenheit, use aluminum foil to line your baking sheet to prevent sticking later on.

- -Slice off your tomatoes' tops then scoop out their innards using a spoon.

- -Crack an egg and pour out the content inside a tomato. Do the same for the remaining tomato and egg.

- -Bake the tomatoes that you've just stuffed with eggs for 30 minutes inside your preheated oven. Remove when done.

- -After the tomatoes have already cooled off, taste them with pepper, salt and parsley.

### 4. Coco Cherridge

Ingredients:

-1 pinch of stevia;

-1/2 cup steel-cut oats;

-3 tablespoons cacao, raw;

-4 cups coconut milk;

-4 tablespoons chia seeds;

-Cherries;

-Coconut shavings;

-Dark chocolate shavings; and

-Maple syrup.

Instructions:

-Mix together the stevia, cacao, coconut milk, chia seeds and steel-cut oats in a saucepan and allow the mixture to boil in medium heat. After it starts to boil, lower heat to simmer until oats get cooked.

-Remove from heat and pour porridge onto a bowl and top it with maple syrup, chocolate shavings, cherries and coconut shavings if desired.

## 5. Quichesparagus

Ingredients:

-1 ½ cups half-half cream;

-1 egg white, beaten lightly;

-1 pound asparagus, sliced into ½ inch pieces;

-1/4 teaspoon nutmeg, ground;

-10 bacon slices;

-2 cups Swiss cheese, shredded;

-2 pie shells, unbaked and 8 inches each;

-4 eggs; and

-Pepper and salt for tasting.

Instructions:

-While preheating your oven to 400 degrees Fahrenheit, steam the asparagus in a covered steamer with about an inch of boiling water for about 2 to 6 minutes or until tender but firm. When done, drain the asparagus and cool.

-Cook the bacon in a deep and big skillet over medium high heat until it becomes evenly browned. After cooking, drain the bacon slices and crumble them before setting aside.

-Take the pie shells and brush them with the beaten egg white and sprinkle both the chopped asparagus and crumbled bacon into them.

-In a mixing bowl, beat the pepper, salt, nutmeg, cream and eggs together.

-Sprinkle the cheese over the asparagus and bacon inside the pie shells and pour the egg mixture over the cheese.

-Bake the pie filled pie shells without cover in the oven for about 35 to 40 minutes or until they become firm. Remove from the oven to cool before enjoying.

## 6. Apple, Rhubarb, and Ginger Muffins

This recipe is a little more in-depth than some of the others that we discuss in this book, but the results are so delicious that it is well-worth the effort!

Ingredients:

- ¼ cup unrefined raw sugar
- ½ cup almond meal
- 1 tablespoon ground linseed meal
- 2 tablespoons finely chopped, crystallized ginger
- ¼ cup fine brown rice flour
- ½ cup buckwheat flour
- 2 teaspoons baking powder
- 2 tablespoons cornflour or arrowroot
- ½ teaspoon ground ginger
- ½ teaspoon ground cinnamon
- Pinch of fine-grain sea salt

- 1 cup rhubarb, finely sliced
- 1 small apple, peeled and cored, finely diced

- 1/3 cup + 1 tablespoon almond or rice milk

- ¼ cup olive oil

- 1 large egg

- 1 teaspoon vanilla extract

Instructions:

- Preheat the oven to 350°F

- Grease eight muffin tins, or line them with paper casings

- Place the almond meal, ginger, sugar, and linseed meal into a medium bowl.

- Using a sieve, add in the flours, spices, and baking powder, then whisk thoroughly.

- Stir in the apple and rhubarb, coating them in the flour mixture.

- In a smaller bowl, whisk together the milk, egg, oil, and vanilla, then pour it into the dry mixture. Stir it all together until just combined.

- Pour the batter into the muffin tins and bake for 20 to 25 minutes or until golden around the edges and a skewer comes out clean when inserted into the center

- Remove from the oven and cool on a wire rack for at least 5 minutes

- These muffins are best when eaten on the same day that they are baked, but they can be stored in an airtight container for up to 3 days, or frozen.

## 7. Ginger and Buckwheat Granola

Ingredients:

- 2 cups oats

- 1 cup buckwheat

- 1 cup pumpkin seeds

- 1 cup sunflower seeds

- 1 ½ cups pitted dates

- 1 cup apple sauce or puree

- 6 tablespoons coconut oil

- 4 tablespoons raw cocoa powder

- Piece of ginger

Instructions:

- Preheat the oven to 350°F

- In a large bowl, thoroughly mix the oats, buckwheat, and the pumpkin and sunflower seeds

- Place the dates, apple sauce or puree, and coconut oil in a sauce pan, and simmer for five minutes until the dates are soft

- While the dates are cooking, peel and grate the ginger, then mix it in with the dates

- Once the dates are soft, place the entire date mixture into a blender with the cocoa powder and blend until completely smooth

- Pour the mixture over the buckwheat, oats, and seed mixture, and stir thoroughly so that everything is coated

- Grease two medium baking trays (or one large baking tray) with coconut oil, then spread the granola out over the tray(s)

- Bake the granola in the oven for about 45 minutes, stirring everything after the first 15 minutes then every 5-10 minutes after that to avoid burning

- Eat right away, or you can store the granola in an airtight container for up to one month

## *8. Berry Crepes*

Ingredients:

- 2 eggs

- 1 teaspoon vanilla

- ½ cup water

- ½ cup almond milk, or other nut milk

- ¼ teaspoon salt

- 1 to 2 tablespoons agave nectar

- 1 cup all-purpose flour

- 2 tablespoons coconut oil, melted

- 1 tablespoon coconut oil for the pan

- 2 cups chopped berries

Instructions:

- In a small saucepan, melt the 2 tablespoons of coconut oil over low heat

- Place the eggs, water, vanilla, nut milk, salt, and agave in a medium mixing bowl, and whisk until combined

- Add the flour in slowly, and whisk to mix

- Remove the oil from the heat and pour it into the batter in a steady stream, whisking slowly

- Mix the combination until it is smooth

- Over medium heat, heat a small amount (~1 tablespoon) of coconut oil in a large frying pan

- Using approximately 1/3 cup per serving, pour the batter onto the frying pan

- As soon as the batter is in the pan, tilt and swirl the pan using a circular motion, making sure that the surface is evenly coated

- Cook for about 2 minutes, until the bottom of the crepe is lightly browned

- Flip with a spatula, and cook the other side

- Continue these steps until you have used all of the batter

## 9. Cinnamon, Apple, and Pear Amaranth Porridge

If you are not familiar with amaranth, you are in for a treat! Amaranth is a type of grain that is a healthy alternative to grits or cream of wheat. It makes a great porridge, and has high levels of fiber and protein. And it is not a starchy or refined grain, so it fits in well with the Anti-Inflammatory Diet.

Ingredients:

- ¼ cup amaranth

- ½ cup unsweetened almond milk (or non-dairy milk of your choice)

- 1 cup filtered water (for cooking, use as much or as little as necessary to get the desired thickness of your porridge)

- ¼ cup pear, diced

- ¼ cup Fuji apple (or other apple of your choice), diced

- 1 tablespoon maple syrup

- 1 tablespoon ground cinnamon

- Dash of freshly ground nutmeg

Instructions:

- Cook the amaranth by bringing water (or non-dairy milk) to a boil. Add the amaranth, reduce to simmer, and cover the pot and cook for 20 minutes. If you need to add more water during the cooking process, the amaranth will continue to absorb the water so that is fine

- In a different saucepan, combine the apples and pears with the cinnamon and maple syrup, and cook the mixture until the fruit is softened, about 10 to 15 minutes

- Stir the stewed apples and pears into the cooked amaranth, and serve hot

## 10. Spanish Frittata

Ingredients:

- 12 large eggs

- ½ cup coconut milk

- ½ teaspoon sea salt, or more to taste

- 2 tablespoons coconut oil or extra-virgin olive oil

- 1 small red onion, finely chopped

- ½ cup sautéed mushrooms (can substitute any vegetable that you desire)

- 1 cup spinach or arugula

Instructions:

- Preheat the oven to 375°F

- Whisk the milk and eggs together in a bowl with 2 pinches of salt

- Over medium-high heat, heat the oil in a pan and add the onions

- Saute the onions until they are translucent, about 3 minutes

- Add the vegetable and sauté until soft

- Add the spinach and fold it into the veggie mixture until it is wilted

- Remove the vegetables from the pan and set them aside

- Turn the heat down to low, and add more oil if necessary

- Using the same pan, add the eggs and shake the pan to make sure that the whole pan is coated

- Cook the eggs over medium-low heat for 5 minutes, until the edges are no longer runny

- Put the vegetable mixture into the pan, distributing it evenly over the egg

- Move the pan to the oven, and cook it for 5 minutes until the dish has set and it is slightly browned

- Remove the dish from the oven, and slide the partially cooked frittata onto a plate from the pan

- Invert the frittata and slide it back into the pan so that the partially cooked side is facing up

- Put the pan back into the oven and cook the dish for another 3 to 4 minutes

- Remove from the oven, and serve warm

## LUNCH RECIPES

### 1. Caulirice

Ingredients:

- Cauliflower, what else?

Instructions:

- Shred your cauliflower into the size of grains using your food processor's shredder blade. If you don't have a food processor, no worries. You can either grate the thing or chop it finely.

- Using a microwavable dish with no water, microwave the shredded cauliflower until fluffy.

- When done, let it cool slightly and eat it, as you would rice.

### 2. Chicken Sesame

Ingredients:

- Chicken filets;

- Spring onions;

- Salt to taste;

- Ginger strips; and

-Sesame oil.

Instructions:

-Boil water in your steamer and while waiting for the water to boil, slather your chicken fillets with salt. Put the chicken fillets in a heat resistant casserole or deep dish.

-Use a fork or a knife to pierce the fillets several times. Sprinkle sesame oil over them and top with ginger strips and spring onions.

-Put the dish or casserole in the steamer and steam for at least 20 minutes with cover after which, remove from heat to let cool before enjoying.

## 3. Wrap-Grilled Salmon

Ingredients:

-1 cup onions, diced;

-1 cup tomatoes, diced;

-Aluminum foil;

-Salmon steaks;

-Some lemon juice; and

-Soy sauce.

Instructions:

-Rub your salmon steaks with some pepper and salt. Wrap each of the steaks in aluminum foil together with some of the chopped tomatoes and onions and grill them up to 10 minutes each side.

-While waiting for the steaks to finish grilling, combine the soy sauce with some lemon juice to achieve your desired sourness level. When done, mix together with the remaining chopped tomatoes and onions.

-Once the salmon steaks are done grilling, remove them from the foils and onto plates. Use the lemon-soy mixture to garnish the steaks for taste.


## 4. Chicken Chili Beans


Ingredients:

-1 cup corn;

-1 pound skinless chicken breast fillets;

-1/8 teaspoon cayenne pepper;

-2 cloves of garlic;

-2 cups natural cheese, grated;

-2 onion, diced;

-2 tablespoons cilantro, chopped;

-2 tablespoons extra-virgin olive oil;

-2 teaspoons chili powder;

-2 teaspoons cumin, ground;

-3 cups water;

-30 ounces canned white beans, rinsed and drained; and

-4 ounces canned green chilies, chopped.

Instructions:

-Use pepper and salt to season the chicken breast fillets.

-Stir-cook the chicken fillets in olive oil over high heat in a big saucepan for up to 3 minutes or until browned.

-Bring the heat down to medium then add in the garlic and onions. Continue cooking for 5 to 6 more minutes or until the onions become translucent.

-Mix the water, spices, chilies, corn and beans in. Let the mixture come to boil, after which bring the heat down to low and allow to simmer for 1 hour without cover.

-Remove from heat and top with cheese and cilantro to enjoy.


## 5. Slow Chili Turkey


Ingredients:

-1 tablespoon chili powder;

-1 tablespoon extra-virgin olive oil;

-1/2 cup frozen corn;

-1/2 onion, diced;

-1/2 pound lean turkey, ground;

-1/2 red pepper, chopped;

-1/2 tablespoon cumin;

-1/2 yellow pepper, chopped;

-15 ounces canned black beans, drained and rinsed;

-15 ounces canned petite tomatoes, diced;

-15 ounces canned red kidney beans, drained and rinsed;

-15 ounces canned tomato sauce;

-8 ounces jar jalapeno peppers, deli-sliced and drained;

-Green onions (optional toppings); and

-Salt and pepper for tasting.

Instructions:

-In a skillet placed over medium heat, cook the turkey in the olive oil until browned. When done, put the turkey in a slow cooker.

-Mix the peppers, onion, diced tomatoes, tomato sauce, jalapenos, beans, chili powder, corn and cumin in. Season with pepper and salt and stir some more.

-Cook on high setting for about 4 hours (or 6 hours if on low setting).

-Top with green onions if desired.


## 6. Coconut Chili Pumpkin Soup

Ingredients:

- 1 medium pumpkin (you can also use butternut squash)
- 1 large white onion, chopped
- 2 garlic cloves, finely chopped
- 1-inch piece of ginger, finely chopped
- ½ chili pepper, seeds removed and chopped
- 4 to 5 sprigs thyme, leaves removed
- 1 1/3 cup coconut milk
- Freshly ground black pepper and sea salt to taste

Instructions:

- Cut the pumpkin in half, then into wedges. Peel each wedge and remove the seeds, then cut the flesh into 1-inch cubes
- Place the pumpkin in a large pan with the garlic, onion, garlic, chili, and thyme
- Pour in about 1 1/3 cup of water, bring to a boil, and cook until the pumpkin turns to pulp
- Add the coconut and season to taste with the black pepper and sea salt
- Reduce the heat and let the soup simmer for 5 to 10 minutes
- Serve hot

## 7. Mediterranean Tuna Salad

Ingredients (makes 2 servings):

- 2 5-ounce cans tuna packed in water
- ¼ cup mayonnaise
- ¼ cup chopped mixed or kalamata olives
- 2 tablespoons red onion, minced
- 2 tablespoons fire-roasted red peppers, chopped
- 2 tablespoons fresh basil, chopped
- 1 tablespoon capers
- 1 tablespoon fresh lemon juice
- Salt and pepper to taste
- 2 large, vine-ripened tomatoes

Instructions:

- Combine all of the ingredients except the tomatoes in a large bowl, and stir to combine
- Without cutting all the way through, slice the tomatoes into sixths then gently open the tomatoes
- Scoop the tuna salad mixture into the tomatoes, and serve!

Note: if you do not like the idea of serving the tuna salad in the tomatoes, it can also be served on a bed of greens, on whole grain bread, or with whole grain crackers.

## 8. Grilled Chicken Wrap with Kale Caesar Salad

Ingredients:

- 8 ounces grilled chicken, thinly sliced
- 1 cup cherry tomatoes, quartered
- 6 cups kale, chopped into bite-sized pieces
- ¾ cup Parmesan cheese, finely shredded
- ½ coddled egg (cooked for about 1 minute)
- 1 garlic clove, minced
- ½ teaspoon Dijon mustard
- 1/8 cup fresh lemon juice
- 1 teaspoon agave or honey
- 1/8 cup olive oil
- Kosher salt and freshly ground black pepper, to taste
- 2 large, whole-grain tortillas

Instructions:

- Mix the egg, garlic, mustard, lemon juice, honey, and olive oil together in a bowl, whisking until it forms a dressing
- Season the dressing with salt and pepper
- Add the chicken, kale, and tomatoes, and toss them until they are coated with the dressing, then cover with ¼ of the shredded Parmesan

- Spread out the tortillas, and evenly distribute the salad

- Sprinkle the remaining ¼ cup Parmesan

- Roll up the wraps, and eat right away


## 9. Sweet Potato and Roasted Red Pepper Soup


Ingredients:

- 2 tablespoons olive oil

- 2 medium onions, chopped

- 12 ounces roasted red peppers, chopped – reserve the liquid

- 4 oz (1 can) green chiles, diced

- 2 teaspoons ground cumin

- 1 teaspoon salt

- 1 teaspoon ground coriander

- 3 to 4 cups sweet potatoes, peeled and cubed

- 4 cups vegetable broth

- 2 tablespoons fresh cilantro, minced

- 1 tablespoon lemon juice

- 4 ounces hard cream cheese, cubed

Instructions:

- Using a large pot or a Dutch oven, heat the olive oil over medium-high heat

- Add the onion, and cook it until it is soft

- Add the red peppers, chiles, cumin, salt, and coriander, and cook for 1 to 2 minutes

- Stir in the juice from the red peppers, along with the sweet potatoes and the vegetable broth

- Bring the mixture to a boil, then reduce the heat and cover, allowing it to simmer

- Cook until the potatoes are tender, approximately 10 to 15 minutes

- Stir in the lemon juice and cilantro, and let the soup cool slightly

- Put half of the soup into a blender and combine it with the cream cheese until the mixture is smooth

- Pour the mixture back into the pot with the remaining soup, and heat thoroughly

## 10. Smoked Salmon and Potato Tartine

Ingredients:

Potato Tartine:

- 1 large russet potato, peeled

- 2 tablespoons neutral flavored oil of your choice

- Salt and pepper to taste

Toppings:

- 4 ounces soft goat cheese, room temperature

- 1 ½ tablespoons chives, finely minced

- ½ garlic clove, finely minced

- Zest of half a lemon

- Smoked salmon, thinly sliced

- 2 tablespoons red onion, finely chopped

- 2 tablespoons capers, drained

- ½ hard-boiled egg, finely chopped

- Additional chives, finely minced, for garnish

Instructions:

Assemble the Toppings:

- In a small bowl, combine the goat cheese with the lemon zest and garlic, season with the salt and pepper, and stir in the 1 ½ tablespoons of chives. Set the bowl aside

- Season the red onion and hard-boiled egg with salt

Prepare Potato Tartine:

- Working quickly to avoid oxidization, grate the potato lengthwise into a large bowl, using the large holes of a grater

- Squeeze the grated potato over the sink to remove any excess liquid

- Season the potato with salt and pepper, and toss to thoroughly mix the spices

- Over medium-high heat, heat the oil in an 8 to 10-inch non-stick skillet

- Once the oil is hot, add the potato and roughly shape it into a large circle

- Press on the potato circle to compact it, then cover the skillet and cook it for 8 to 10 minutes or until the bottom is golden brown

- Carefully flip the potato circle and cook the other side for another 8 to 10 minutes or until each side is golden brown

- Remove the potato from the skillet and place it on a rack to cool until it is room temperature

Assemble Tartine:

- When the potato cake has cooled, spread the goat cheese mixture over the top of the cake

- Layer the smoked salmon directly over the cream cheese, and sprinkle on the red onion, egg, and capers

- Cut into wedges, garnish with the additional fresh chives, and serve immediately


## 11. Squash and Red Lentil Curry Stew


Ingredients:

- 1 teaspoon extra-virgin olive oil

- 1 sweet onion, chopped

- 3 garlic cloves, minced

- 1 tablespoon curry powder (or more to taste)

- 1 carton (4 cups) broth

- 1 cup red lentils

- 3 cups butternut squash, cooked

- 1 cup greens of choice (kale, spinach are best)

- Fresh ginger, grated, to taste (optional)

- Salt and black pepper, to taste

Instructions:

- In a large pot, heat the oil and then add the onion and garlic. Saute over medium-low heat for about 5 minutes

- Stir in the curry powder, and cook for another 2 or 3 minutes

- Add the broth and lentils and bring the mixture to a boil, then reduce heat and simmer for 10 minutes

- Stir in the butternut squash and greens, and cook over medium heat for another 5 to 8 minutes

- Season with salt, pepper, and ginger (if desired), to taste

- Serve hot


## *12. Winter Fruit Salad*

Ingredients:

Salad:

- 4 Fuyu persimmons (or enough to make 2 cups), cut into 1-inch cubes

- 3 Bosch pears (or enough to make 2 cups), cut into 1-inch cubes

- 1 cup grapes, halved or quartered

- ¾ cup pecans, halved lengthwise to make slivers

Note: you can use other fruits like figs, apples, or pomegranate arils, as long as you make sure that you have 5 to 6 cups of fruit in total

Dressing:

- 1 tablespoon extra-virgin olive oil – you may want to use one that is fruity-flavored for added flavor

- 1 tablespoon peanut oil

- 1 tablespoon pomegranate-flavored vinegar

- 2 tablespoons agave nectar

Instructions:

- Whisk the dressing ingredients together so that the flavors can mix while you cut the fruit

- Place the cut fruit into a large bowl

- Toss the fruit with the dressing

- Right before serving, toss the salad with the pecan slivers

# DINNER RECIPES

## 1. Stoned Salmon Poach

Ingredients:

For The Salmon:

-10 black peppercorns;

-2 limes, sliced thinly;

-4 pieces of quarter pound wild salmon;

-6 cups seafood stock;

-Juice of 2 limes; and

-Pepper and salt.

For The Chutney

-1 onion, chopped finely;

-1 teaspoon dried lavender;

-1/3 cup red wine vinegar;

-1/4 teaspoon chili flakes;

-2 pounds of small stone fruit, diced;

-2 tablespoons garlic, minced;

-3/4 cup agave;

-3/4 teaspoon salt; and

-Zest of 1 lime or lemon.

Instructions:

For The Poached Salmon:

-Put the peppercorns, limes and seafood stock in a heavy pot on high heat and allow to boil. When it begins to boil, bring the heat down to simmer with cover for 5 minutes.

-Use pepper and salt to season the salmon. Lower the seasoned salmon pieces in the simmering liquid in the heavy pot until at least ¾ of the salmon pieces are covered in liquid. Then, bring the heat down further to reduce to a gentle simmer and continue cooking for 6 more minutes or until the salmon pieces turn opaque and you can already flake them with a fork.

-When done, remove the salmon and set them aside on a plate lined with towels.

For The Chutney:

-Except for the herbs, combine all the chutney's other ingredients and bring to boil and continue doing so for 15 minutes with occasional stirring. Then, mix the lavender and fresh herbs in.

-Top the poached salmon with the chutney to enjoy.

## 2. Potato Egg Curry

Ingredients:

-1 tablespoon extra-virgin olive oil;

-15 ounces canned tomato sauce;

-2 garlic cloves;

-2 russet potatoes;

-2 tablespoons curry powder;

-4 eggs;

-An inch of fresh ginger;

-Half a bunch of fresh cilantro (optional);

Instructions:

-Cut the potatoes in to cubes about ¾ inch each in size after washing them. Boil the potatoes in a large pot over high heat for up to 6 minutes or until they become tender as you pierce them with a fork. When done, use a colander to drain the potatoes.

-As the potatoes are boiling, start making the sauce. After peeling the ginger, grate about an inch's worth of it and mince the garlic.

-In a deep and large skillet, sauté the garlic and ginger in extra-virgin olive oil on medium low heat for up to 2 minutes or until they turn fragrant and soft. Mix the curry powder in and continue sautéing for another minute for the spices to roast.

-Mix in the tomato sauce and combine by stirring. Bring the heat up to medium to heat through the sauce. Add salt if after tasting, you think it's needed.

-Mix the cooked potatoes in and coat with the sauce by stirring. Put several teaspoons of water if you think the mixture is pasty or rather dry.

-In the potato mixture, dig 4 tiny wells and in each, crack an egg. Cover the skillet and allow the mixture to simmer the eggs for up to 10 minutes or until the eggs are cooked through.

-Enjoy with cilantro toppings if desired.

### 3. *Sweetatotata ConSalsa*

Ingredients:

Frittata

   -1 big sweet potato;

   -1 shallot, minced and peeled;

   -1 tablespoon extra-virgin olive oil;

   -4 big eggs;

   -A handful of chives, snipped finely; and

   -Salt and pepper for tasting.

Tomato Salsa

   -1 dash Tabasco sauce;

   -1 pinch sugar (optional);

   -1 tablespoon sesame oil;

   -2 green onions, thinly and diagonally sliced;

   -3 tablespoons extra-virgin olive oil;

   -8 ounces plum tomatoes;

-A handful of cilantro leaves, chopped;

-Juice of half a lemon;

Instructions:

For The Salsa:

-Slice the tomatoes into quarters and put them in a big bowl. Mix the other salsa ingredients well and taste with pepper and salt. Use a bit of sugar if desired.

For The Frittata:

-Bring your broiler to its highest temperature setting. While waiting, peel your sweet potatoes and slice them into cubes about ½ inch in size.

-Cook the sweet potato cubes and shallots in the extra-virgin olive oil in an omelet pan or skillet – seasoned with pepper and salt – over medium heat for about 5 minutes with occasional turning or until the turn tender and slightly golden on the edges.

-Lightly beat the eggs in a bowl before adding the chives in. Pour the mixture on the sweet potatoes, gently shaking the pan to gently spread the ingredients. Continue cooking – don't stir – for a few minutes more or until the eggs tart settling at the bottom and the sides.

-Bring the pan beneath the hot broiler for a short while or until the top part of the frittata has already set. Be careful not to overcook your eggs lest they become rubbery in texture.

-When done, let it stand for about a minute before running a heatproof spatula around the frittata's sides so you can invert it on a big plate.

-Top the frittata with the tomato salsa to enjoy.

### 4. Salmon Chowder

Ingredients:

-1 celery, diced;

-1 liter of chicken stock;

-1 tablespoon extra-virgin coconut oil;

-1 teaspoon parsley, dried;

-1/2 onion, sliced;

-1/2 teaspoon curry powder;

-2 cloves of garlic, chopped;

-2 pieces turnips, skins removed and sliced into cubes;

-250 ml pure and natural coconut milk;

-4 skinless and boneless salmon fillets;

-pepper and salt for tasting; and

-Italian flat-leaf parsley for serving (garnishing).

Instructions:

-In a big frying pan, melt ½ tablespoon of coconut oil in medium heat to cook the salmon for 3 minutes per side or until cooked. Put aside when done and allow to cool enough to be handled and flaked into pieces.

-In a big saucepan on medium heat, melt the remaining ½ tablespoon of coconut oil and in it, stir fry the curry powder, celery, garlic and onion for up to 4 minutes or until the onions become translucent. Mix parsley, turnip and stock in and cook for another 20 minutes with over or just until the turnip turns soft.

-Mix the coconut milk in and combine by stirring.

-Remove from heat to let the mixture cool slightly before pouring it into a blender or food processor together with your flaked salmon. Puree the mixture until smooth.

-Season with pepper and slat to taste and if desired, garnish with parsley.


## 5. Nutty Quinoa Salad


Ingredients:

For The Quinoa:

-1 avocado, thinly sliced or chopped;

-1 cup carrots, chopped finely;

-1 cup cashews, chopped coarsely;

-1 cup quinoa, rinsed well and dried;

-1 not overly ripe mango, chopped;

-1 tablespoon extra-virgin olive oil;

-1/2 inch ginger, chopped finely;

-1/2 onion, chopped finely;

-1/4 cup fresh mint, chopped finely;

-2 tablespoons agave;

-3 cups lettuce, chopped roughly;

-Juice of 1 lime; and

-Salt and pepper to taste.

Instructions:

-Boil 2 cups of water in a medium-sized saucepan and add the quinoa. Simmer for 15 to 20 minutes with cover or until the quinoa has fully absorbed the water. Set aside to cool.

-While waiting for your quinoa to cool, toss together the carrots and red onion.

-In a separate bowl, whisk the olive oil, agave and lime juice then add the mixture to the bowl containing the tossed onion and carrots.

-Mix in the cooled quinoa and mango and toss everything well. Add in the ginger, cilantro and mint and mix well. Taste with pepper and salt. Garnish with the cashews and avocado slices.

-To the lettuce with scoops of the mixture and enjoy either chilled or at room temperature.

## *6. Baked Tilapia Topped With Pecan Rosemary*

Ingredients:

- 1/3 cup raw pecans, chopped

- 1/3 cup panko breadcrumbs

- 2 teaspoons fresh rosemary, chopped

- ½ teaspoon brown sugar, packed

- 1/8 teaspoon salt

- 1 pinch cayenne pepper

- 1 ½ teaspoon extra-virgin olive oil

- 1 egg white

- 4 tilapia filets (approximately 4 ounces each)

Instructions:

- Preheat the oven to 350°F

- Stir together the pecans, breadcrumbs, sugar, salt, and cayenne pepper in a small baking dish

- Add the olive oil and toss the pecan mixture so it is coated with the oil

- Bake the mixture until it is a light golden brown, approximately 7 to 8 minutes

- Increase the heat to 400°F

- Grease a large glass baking dish with cooking spray

- In a shallow dish, whisk the egg white

- Dip each tilapia filet in the egg white, one filet at a time, then dip each filet into the pecan mixture so that each side is coated

- Place the filets into the baking dish

- Take the remaining pecan mixture and press it into the tops of the tilapia filets

- Bake the filets until the tilapia is just cooked through, around 10 minutes

- Serve hot


### 7. Italian Stuffed Red Peppers

Ingredients:

- 1 lb lean ground turkey

- 3 red bell peppers

- 2 cups spaghetti sauce

- 1 teaspoon Italian herb blend (oregano, basil, etc.)

- 1 teaspoon garlic powder, or 1 garlic clove, pressed

- ½ teaspoon each of salt and pepper

- ½ cup frozen chopped spinach or other dark leafy green of choice

- 8 tablespoons Parmesan cheese, grated – 2 tablespoons for the recipe, and 6 for garnish per pepper half

Instructions:

- Preheat the oven to 450°F

- Line a baking sheet with foil, and coat the foil with a non-stick cooking spray

- Wash the peppers, and remove the stem

- Cut the peppers in half length-wise and remove the seeds and ribs

- Place the peppers on the baking sheet

- Over medium-high heat, cook the turkey in a large, non-stick skillet or frying pan

- Break up and stir the turkey while it is cooking

- When the turkey is almost completely cooked, add the sauce and seasonings to the skillet or pan

- Stir the turkey mixture and keep cooking until the turkey is thoroughly cooked (no longer pink)

- Add the spinach (or leafy green of your choice) and 2 tablespoons of Parmesan cheese, and stir until the mixture is well-combined

- Scoop ½ cup of the turkey mixture into each pepper half

- Sprinkle 1 tablespoon of Parmesan cheese over each pepper half

- Bake for 20 to 30 minutes, or until the cheese is melted and lightly golden brown

- Serve hot

## 8. Lemon Herb Salmon and Zucchini

The great thing about this recipe is that it is all made in one pan, meaning that it is easy to make and to clean up after!

Ingredients:

Zucchini:

- 2 tablespoons extra-virgin olive oil

- 4 zucchini, chopped

- Salt and pepper, to taste

Salmon:

- 4 salmon filets, about 5 ounces each

- 2 tablespoons brown sugar, packed

- 2 tablespoons lemon juice, freshly squeezed

- 1 tablespoon Dijon mustard

- 2 garlic cloves, minced

- ½ teaspoon dried oregano

- ½ teaspoon dried dill

- ¼ teaspoon dried rosemary

- ¼ teaspoon dried thyme

- Salt and pepper, to taste

- 2 tablespoons fresh parsley, chopped, for garnish

Instructions:

- Preheat the oven to 400°F

- Lightly cover a baking sheet with oil, or use a non-stick cooking spray

- Whisk the brown sugar, lemon juice, mustard, garlic, oregano, dill, rosemary, and thyme together in a small bowl. Season with salt and pepper, to taste, and set aside

- Place the zucchini onto the baking sheet in a single layer

- Drizzle the zucchini with olive oil and season with salt and pepper, to taste

- Add the salmon, also in a single layer, and brush each filet with the herb mixture from the bowl

- Place the baking sheet in the oven and cook about 16 to 18 minutes or until the fish is easily flaked with a fork

- Serve immediately, garnished with parsley


## 9. Sweet Potato and Black Bean Burgers with Avocado-Cilantro Crema

Ingredients:

Burgers:

- ½ cup quinoa

- 1 can black beans, drained and rinsed

- 1 large sweet potato

- 2 garlic cloves, minced

- ½ cup red onion, diced

- ½ cup cilantro, chopped

- ½ jalapeno pepper, seeded and diced

- 2 teaspoons spicy Cajun seasoning

- 1 teaspoon cumin

- 1/3 cup oat flour or oat bran

- Extra-virgin olive oil or coconut oil for cooking

- 6 whole-grain hamburger buns

Avocado-Cilantro Crema:

- ½ large ripe avocado, diced

- ¼ cup plain greek yogurt or low-fat sour cream

- 2 tablespoons chopped cilantro

- 1 teaspoon lime juice

- Dash of hot sauce (optional)

- Salt, to taste

Instructions:

Quinoa:

- Rinse the quinoa in cold water in a mesh strainer

- Bring 1 cup of cold water to boil in a medium saucepan

- Add the quinoa, bring the water to a boil again

- Cover the pan, reduce the heat to low and simmer for 15 minutes or until the quinoa has absorbed all the water

- Remove the pan from the heat and fluff the quinoa, then place it in a large bowl and let it cool for about 10 minutes

Burgers:

- Poke the sweet potato with a fork several times and cook it in the microwave for about 3 to 4 minutes or until it is cooked through and soft (make sure not to overcook it, or it will harden)

- Alternative: roast the sweet potato in the oven at 400°F for 30 minutes

- When the sweet potato is done cooking, remove the skin and allow the potato to cool

- Using a food processor or strong blender, combine the beans, sweet potato, onion, garlic, cilantro, Cajun seasoning, and cumin, and blend on pulse until the mixture is almost smooth

- Move the mixture to the bowl with the quinoa, and add salt and pepper to taste

- Mix in the oat flour/oat bran, just enough to enable you to shape the patties and have them stick together

- Divide the mixture into 6 patties (about ½ cup each) and put the patties on parchment paper on a baking sheet

- Refrigerate the patties for at least 30 minutes to help them stick together

- After 30 minutes, heat the oil in a skillet over medium-high heat

- Fry the burgers for about 3 to 4 minutes per side, or until each side is golden brown

Avocado-Cilantro Crema:

- Using the food processor or blender, combine the sour cream or yogurt, avocado, cilantro, and lime juice, and blend until smooth, adding salt to taste

- Place the crema in the refrigerator until the burgers are ready to serve, then top the burgers with the crema

## 10. Quinoa and Turkey Stuffed Bell Peppers

Ingredients:

- 3 large yellow peppers

- 1 ¼ lb extra-lean ground turkey

- 1 cup mushrooms, diced

- ¼ cup sweet onion, diced

- 1 cup fresh spinach, chopped

- 2 teaspoons garlic, minced

- 1 (8 oz) can tomato sauce

- 1 cup chicken broth

- 1 cup dry quinoa

- 1 tablespoon extra-virgin olive oil

Instructions:

- Preheat the oven to 400°F

- Using a small saucepan, cook the quinoa according to the package directions (about 15 minutes)

- While the quinoa is cooking, heat the oil in a frying pan over medium heat, and sauté the vegetables for about 5 minutes

- Add the turkey and garlic to the vegetables, and continue cooking over medium heat

- When the turkey is mostly cooked, add the tomato sauce and half of the broth

- Allow the mixture to simmer until the turkey is fully cooked and you have cooked off some of the excess liquid

- While the turkey is simmering, prepare the bell peppers: cut them in half, removing the stem and seeds

- Spray a 9 x 13 baking pan with cooking spray and put the bell peppers open side up into the baking pan

- When the quinoa is done cooking, put it into the frying pan with the turkey and vegetables, and stir it all together

- Divide the turkey mixture evenly between the bell pepper halves, scooping the mixture into the peppers

- Pour the remaining chicken broth into the base of the baking pan (around the peppers, not on top of them)

- Cover the baking pan with foil and bake for about 30 to 35 minutes

- Serve hot

## 11. Indian Spiced Carrot Soup With Ginger

Ingredients:

- 1 teaspoon coriander seeds

- ½ teaspoon yellow mustard seeds

- 3 tablespoons walnut oil

- ½ teaspoon curry powder

- 1 tablespoon fresh ginger, peeled and minced

- 2 cups onions, chopped

- 1 ½ lbs carrots (about 4 cups), peeled and sliced into thin rounds

- 1 ½ teaspoons lime peel, finely grated

- 5 cups low-sodium chicken or vegetable broth

- 2 teaspoons fresh lime juice

Instructions:

- Grind the coriander and mustard seeds to a fine powder

- Heat the oil in a large pot over medium-high heat

- Add the ground coriander and mustard and the curry powder, and stir for 1 minute

- Add the ginger and stir for another minute

- Add the onions, carrots, and lime peel, and sprinkle with salt and pepper to taste

- Saute until the onions start to soften, about 3 minutes

- Add the broth and bring the mixture to a boil

- Reduce the heat to medium-low and simmer uncovered for about 30 minutes or until the carrots are tender

- Allow the soup to cool slightly

- Working in batches, puree the soup in a blender until it is completely smooth

- Put the soup back in the pot, and add soup ¼ a cup at a time if the mixture is too thick

- Stir in the lime juice, season with salt and pepper

- Serve warm, or prepare the day before and serve cold

## 12. Roasted Root Vegetables

Ingredients:

- 1 large butternut squash, peeled, seeded, and cut into ½-inch pieces (about 5 cups)

- 1 ½ lbs Yukon Gold potatoes, unpeeled, cut into ½-inch pieces

- 1 bunch beets (about 1 ½ lbs), trimmed not peeled, scrubbed, cut into ½-inch pieces

- 1 medium red onion, cut into ½-inch pieces (about 2 cups)

- 1 large turnip, peeled, cut into ½-inch pieces (about 1 cup)

- 1 head of garlic, cloves separated and peeled

- 2 tablespoons extra-virgin olive oil

Instructions:

- Preheat the oven to 425°F

- Grease 2 large, rimmed baking sheets

- In a large bowl, combine all of the ingredients and toss them to coat with the oil

- Sprinkle salt and pepper over the mixture, to taste

- Roast the vegetables for about 1 hour and 15 minutes or until the vegetables are tender and golden brown

- If you need to reheat the vegetables, do so for 15 minutes at 350°F

## DESSERTS

### *1. Anti Inflammatory Rice Pudding*

Ingredients:

- -1 cup of pure coconut milk, unsweetened;

- -1/2 cup brown rice;

- -1/3 cup raisins;

- -1/4 cup brown rice syrup;

- -1/4 teaspoon cardamom, ground;

- -1/4 teaspoon ginger, ground;

- -1/8 teaspoon black pepper;

- -1/8 teaspoon cinnamon;

- -1/8 teaspoon turmeric; and

- -2 cups of rice milk.

Instructions:

- -In a medium-sized pot over medium-high heat, mix together the coconut and rice milks and bring to a boil. Mix the rice in and bring it back to a boil then lower the heat to cook and simmer for 30 minutes with cover.

- -Mix the spices in and cook for 15 more minutes with cover until the rice is cooked.

-After cooking the rice, mix in the raisins and the brown rice syrup. Let the rice cool in the fridge for a few hours before enjoying.

-You can garnish with a drop or two of vanilla extract or cashews if you desire.

## 2. Applesauce Quinoa Crepes

Ingredients:

-1 ½ cups quinoa flour;

-1 teaspoon baking soda;

-1 teaspoon cinnamon;

-2 cups carbonated water;

-3 tablespoons extra-virgin oil;

-3 cups unsweetened applesauce;

-1/2 cup tapioca flour; and

-Cinnamon for tasting.

Instructions:

-Combine the cinnamon, baking soda, tapioca flour and quinoa flour in a medium-sized bowl. When done, mix in the oil and water – whisk to combine well.

-Heat a big skillet – preferably non-stick – over medium heat and place a couple of drops of the oil.

-Make the first crepe by pouring 1/3 cup of the mixture in the skillet. Rotate the skillet fast to evenly coat the bottom with the mixture. Cook the crepe in the skillet at medium high heat until its bottom becomes light brown before flipping over to cook the other side briefly.

-Do the same with the remaining batter until all used up. Enjoy with applesauce.


### 3. Anti-Inflammatory Key Lime Pudding


Ingredients:

-1/3 cup agave, more for tasting;

-1/2 cup fresh lemon juice;

-1/2 cup fresh lime juice;

-2 ripe avocados, peeled and pitted;

-2 cups bananas, chopped;

-1 teaspoon lemon zest, finely grated;

-1 teaspoon lime zest, finely grated;

Instructions:

-Throw everything in the blender to puree for 1 to minutes at high speed or until all's been combined well. To ensure even mixing, I highly recommend stopping the machine once in a while to scrape down the sides.

-Adjust your sweetener (agave) for taste.

-Split the pureed mixture among 4 glasses to refrigerate for 3 hours in order to thicken. To avoid oxidation, serve the pudding chilled and on the same day.

## 4. Dark Gingermeric Choco Maple Cups

Ingredients:

### For The Chocolate:

-1 pinch salt;

-1 teaspoon ginger, grated finely;

-1 teaspoon turmeric, ground;

-1/2 cup and 2 tablespoons coconut sugar, finely powdered;

-1/2 teaspoon ginger, ground;

-140 grams cacao butter;

-3/4 cup cacao powder, sifted;

### For The Filling:

-1/2 cup cashews, raw and soaked overnight, drained and rinsed;

-1/4 cup virgin coconut oil, melted;

-3 tablespoons maple syrup;

-3 tablespoons orange juice, freshly squeezed;

-1 teaspoon orange zest and extra for optional garnishing;

Instructions:

-Use 12 silicone baking cups to line a muffin tin.

-Blend the soaked cashews, maple syrup, melted coconut oil, orange juice and 1 teaspoon of orange zest in a processor or blender for about 30 seconds or until smooth to make the cream filling.

-Pour the mixture onto a small bowl and leave in the freezer to allow it to firm up a little, e.g., custard-like consistency.

-While chilling the cream filling, make the chocolate by melting the cacao butter in a medium-sized saucepan over the lowest heat setting from 5 to 15 minutes.

-While waiting for the butter to melt, whisk together the coconut sugar, cacao powder, salt, turmeric and ginger in a separate bowl. Whisk the mixture in once the cacao butter has fully melted. Make all are well combined.

-Turn the heat off. Place about ¾ to 1 tablespoon of the chocolate mixture in each of the silicone baking cups. Mix the melted chocolate every now and then to prevent the ingredients from separating.

-Leave the muffin pan with the cups inside the freezer for up to 10 minutes to let the chocolate become a little firm. After it becomes generally solid, top each of the chocolate cups with up to a tablespoon of the cream filling.

-Finish each of the cups by topping with up to 1 tablespoon of the remaining chocolate and put them back in the freezer for another 5 minutes, after which top with the remaining orange zest before freezing for at least 2 hours to solidify the fillings.

-Once they're already solid, pop them out of the silicone cups to transfer to a container for storage in the fridge or freezer.

## 5. *Banana Buckrepes*

Ingredients:

-1 ¼ cups rice milk

-1 tablespoon extra-virgin olive oil and extra for frying;

-1/2 teaspoon salt;

-1/3 cup quinoa flour;

-2 big bananas, sliced;

-2 eggs;

-2/3 cup buckwheat flour; and

-Brown rice syrup for serving.

Instructions:

-In a medium-sized bowl, beat the eggs and mix the rice milk, quinoa flour, buckwheat flour, extra-virgin olive oil and salt in, whisking until all have been combined well.

-Preheat a big skillet on medium heat and spray with the remaining extra-virgin olive oil to prepare for cooking the crepes.

-Pour 1/3 cup of the mixture on the skillet and quickly rotate so that the bottom will be evenly coated with the mixture. On medium-high heat, cook the crepe for up to 2 minutes or until bubbles start appearing. Flip the crepe over to cook for up to 60 seconds more before removing from the skillet. Do the same for the remaining batter until fully used up.

-Enjoy your crepes with brown rice syrup and sliced bananas.


## 6. Pumpkin Chocolate Chip Cookies

Ingredients:

Wet Ingredients:

- 2 large eggs

- ½ cup pumpkin or squash pulp, cooked and drained

- ½ teaspoon maple flavoring

- 1 tablespoon pure vanilla extract

- 1 ½ cups raw honey

- 1 cup coconut butter

Dry Ingredients:

- 1 cup almond meal or almond flour

- 3 tablespoons arrowroot flour

- ½ teaspoon unprocessed salt

- 1 tablespoon pumpkin pie spice

- 1 ½ cups nuts, coarsely chopped

- 1 cup dark chocolate baking chips

Instructions:

- Preheat the oven to 350°F

- Line two baking sheets with parchment paper

- Using a food processor or a mixer, combine the eggs, pumpkin, vanilla, maple, and sweetener, and mix until completely liquefied

- Add the coconut butter and mix again until completely smooth

- Add the almond meal or flour, arrowroot, salt, and pumpkin pie spice, and mix well

- If the dough begins to fall apart, add more almond meal or arrowroot until the dough sticks together

- Once mixed, add in the nuts and pulse briefly so that the nuts are still in fairly large pieces

- Put the dough into a bowl and chill it for about 15 minutes

- Remove the dough from the refrigerator, and stir in the chocolate chips

- Spoon 1-inch round portions of dough onto the cookie sheets

- Grease your palms with coconut oil and press the dough portions flat with your hands

- Bake for 18 to 20 minutes, until the cookies are just browned on the edges

- Remove the cookies from the oven, allow them to cool on the baking sheets, and then enjoy!


## 7. Apple Raspberry Crumble


Ingredients:

- 5 large cooking apples, finely sliced

- 1 cup raspberries

- 2 cups rolled oats

- 2 cups apple juice

- 2 tablespoons brown sugar

- 2 tablespoons non-dairy butter

- 2 teaspoons cinnamon

- ½ teaspoon cloves

Instructions:

- Preheat the oven to 350°F

- Grease a baking dish and place the apple slices and raspberries into the dish

- Pour the apple juice over the apples and raspberries

- In a medium-sized bowl, mix the oats, sugar, and spices

- Cut in the butter with your fingers until it is evenly dispersed

- Cover the apples and raspberries with the crumble topping

- Bake the crumble for 45 to 60 minutes

- Serve hot or cold, depending on your preference

## 8. Grilled Fruit

This recipe involves any anti-inflammatory fruits that you would like to eat, but tastes extra sweet because the grilling caramelizes the natural sugars in the fruit and reduces the water content which concentrates the flavor.

Ingredients:

- Sliced pineapple, banana, pear, and/or apple, in whichever portions you would like to eat

Instructions:

- Turn on the grill and cook the fruit until it is thoroughly grilled

## 9. Dark Chocolate Bark

Ingredients:

- 1 bar of dark chocolate

- Seeds (sunflower, pumpkin) and berries as desired

Instructions:

- Melt the dark chocolate in the microwave or on the stove, then spread it on parchment paper

- Sprinkle the berries and seeds over top of the chocolate

- Refrigerate the bark until thoroughly chilled, then serve

## SNACK RECIPES

### 1. Cauli-Turmeric Roast

Ingredients:

-1 pinch of black cumin;

-1 tablespoon and 1 head of cauliflower;

-1 tablespoon turmeric; and

-Pepper and salt for optional tasting.

Instructions:

-Begin by preheating the oven to 400 degrees Fahrenheit.

-Chop the cauliflower head into small florets and place them inside a standard-sized baking dish. Mix the black cumin, turmeric, salt and a bit of olive oil in. Toss everything well.

-Cover the dish with foil to keep the florets from drying. Put the baking dish inside the preheated oven to bake for 40 minutes. Remove the foil and continue baking for 15 minutes more.


## 2. Anti-Inflammatory Seed Snacks


Ingredients:

-1/2 teaspoon garlic;

-1/4 teaspoon turmeric powder;

-1/8 teaspoon black pepper;

-Squash or pumpkin seeds, freshly scooped; and

-Salt for optional tasting.

Instructions:

-While preheating your oven to 275 degrees Fahrenheit, rinse and dry off the seeds to remove the stringy stuff.

-Inside a bag, combine all the ingredients and shake well. Ensure the seeds are well coated and add some oil if you like.

-Line a baking sheet with parchment paper and spread the coated seeds on it. Bake in the preheated oven for up to 25 minutes or until they taste like crunchy popcorn.

### 3. Bugs Bunny's Anti-Inflammatory Cake

Ingredients:

-1 ½ cup whole-wheat flour;

-1 cup honey, microwaved for 30 seconds;

-1 cup unbleached white flour;

-1 teaspoon cinnamon;

-1/2 cup pineapple, chopped and drained;

-1/2 teaspoon allspice, ground;

-1/4 cup extra-virgin olive oil;

-2 cups carrots, finely grated;

-2 teaspoons baking soda;

-2 teaspoons vanilla extract;

-3/4 cup walnuts, chopped; and

-Juice of a big orange.

Instructions:

-While preheating your oven to 350 degrees Fahrenheit, combine the orange juice, carrots, olive oil, vanilla, pineapple and honey until blended well.

-In a separate bowl, mix the spices, baking soda and flours together. Add in the walnuts before adding the mixture into the carrot mixture. Continue stirring until mixed well.

-Empty the batter into an 8-inch square non-stick baking pan. Bake in the preheated oven from 45 to 60 minutes or until it passes the knife test, i.e., a knife inserted at the center will come out clean.

-Take the pan out of the oven to slightly cool before removing from the pan to enjoy.

## 4. Anti-Inflammatory Muffins of Love

Ingredients:

-1 big egg;

-1 cup blueberries;

-1 cup whole wheat flour;

-1/2 teaspoon baking powder;

-1/3 cup brown sugar;

-1/3 cup cashews, chopped;

-1/4 cup almond milk; and

-1/4 teaspoon salt.

Instructions:

-While preheating your oven to 350 degrees Fahrenheit, mix the slat, cashews, baking powder, sugar and flour. In another mixing bowl, beat the egg and milk together before combining with the dry ingredients in the other bowl. Mix well.

-Pour the mixture into paper muffin cups and bake in your preheated oven for from 30 to 40 minutes before transferring to cool slightly on a wire rack.

-Best enjoyed warm.

## 5. Wholewheat Bananutty Muffins

Ingredients:

-1 cup whole-wheat flour;

-1 egg, beaten lightly;

-1/2 teaspoon baking powder;

-1/3 cup brown sugar;

-1/4 cup almond milk;

-1/4 teaspoon salt;

-2 bananas, chopped; and

-2/3 cup walnuts, chopped.

Instructions:

-While preheating your oven to 350 degrees Fahrenheit, mix the walnuts, salt, sugar, flour and baking powder. In another bowl, use a fork to mash the banana cuts.

-Add in the egg and almond milk to the mashed banana followed by the dry ingredients mixture. Mix together well before pouring it in a non-stick muffin pan.

-Bake in your preheated oven for 30 to 40 minutes. Remove from the oven to cool on a wire rack before enjoying warm.

## 6. *Krispy Kale Chips*

If you have tried kale chips before and did not enjoy them, give them another chance. The most important part of a kale chip recipe is making sure that the kale chips come out nice and crispy; mushy kale chips are particularly unappetizing. If the time set out in the recipe does not end up working with your oven, experiment to see how long you need to leave the chips in to get them nice and crispy. I promise that when you figure out that perfect balance, you will understand just how awesome kale chips can be! You can also add a little bit of hot sauce to your chips when serving them; hot sauce and kale makes a delightful combination.

Ingredients:

- 1 bunch of kale

- 1 tablespoon olive oil

- 1 teaspoon salt

- Black pepper to taste

- Ground garlic to taste (optional)

Instructions:

- Preheat the oven to 350°F

- Line a baking sheet with parchment paper

- Using a knife or kitchen shears, remove the kale leaves from the stems and tear the leaves into bite-sized pieces

- Wash the kale and dry it thoroughly using a salad spinner. This step is very important in getting the kale crispy, because excess liquid will cause it to be mushy

- Place the kale in a bowl, and drizzle it with the olive oil and whichever seasonings you are using

- Massage the oil and seasoning into the kale, making sure that it is evenly coated

- Place the kale in a thin layer on the baking sheet, and bake 10 to 15 minutes

## 7. Citrus Salad With Ginger Yogurt

Ingredients:

- 1 pink grapefruit, peeled

- 2 large tangerines, peeled

- 3 navel oranges

- ½ cup dried cranberries

- 2 tablespoons honey

- ¼ teaspoon ground cinnamon

- 1 16-ounce container low-fat Greek yogurt

- ¼ cup golden brown sugar

- 2/3 cup minced crystallized ginger
- Dried cranberries to garnish

Instructions:

- Break the tangerines and grapefruit into sections
- Cut the grapefruit sections into thirds, and the tangerine sections in half
- Put the grapefruit, tangerines, and all of their juices into a deep serving bowl
- Using a small and sharp knife, cut all of the peel and white pith from the oranges
- Slice the oranges into 1/4-inch thick rounds, then quarter those
- Add the oranges and their juices to the bowl with the grapefruit and tangerines
- Add in the 1/2 cup of dried cranberries, cinnamon, and honey
- Cover the mixture and refrigerate it for at least 1 hour
- Mix the yogurt and ginger in a bowl, cover, and chill alongside the fruit mixture
- Once chilled, spoon the yogurt onto the fruit, and sprinkle with brown sugar and the extra dried cranberries

## 8. Apple Slices With Cinnamon

This recipe is very easy to make and is extremely basic, but it is also delicious and provides a good anti-inflammation boost. It is a great mid-day snack option.

Ingredients:

- 1 medium apple, cored and sliced

- ¼ teaspoon ground cinnamon

Instructions:

- Sprinkle the apple slices with cinnamon and eat while the apple is still fresh

## SHAKES AND SMOOTHIES

## 1. Froaty (Fruits and Oats) Shake

Ingredients:

-1 Banana;

-1 cup low fat vanilla yogurt;

-1 cup strawberries;

-1/2 cup steel-cut oats;

-1/4 cup almonds;

-3 ice cubes; and

-Water.

Instructions:

-Simply blend all the ingredients using a processor or blender until you achieve a smooth consistency.


## 2. A Berry Gingery Anti-Inflammation Smoothie


Ingredients:

-1 cup celery;

-1 cup strawberries;

-1 piece of ginger, 2 inches long and peeled;

-2 cup of kale;

-3 tablespoons protein powder;

-Water.

Instructions:

-Simply blend everything in a food processor or blender until you achieve a smooth consistency and enjoy immediately.


## 3. Tropical Anti-Inflammatory Smoothie


Ingredients:

-1 ½ cups pineapple, chopped;

-1 cup unsweetened almond milk;

-1 frozen banana;

-1 orange, peeled and chopped roughly;

-1 small thumb of ginger;

-1 tablespoon chia seeds; and

-1 teaspoon turmeric, ground.

Instructions:

-Simply puree everything in a processor or blender until you achieve a relatively creamy and smooth consistency.

## 4. Proteinutty Shake

Ingredients:

-1/8 cup walnuts;

-½ cup blueberries;

-1 cup pure coconut milk;

-1 tablespoon honey;

-1/4 cup steel-cut oats;

-1 tablespoon flax seed; and

-1 banana.

Instructions:

-Blend everything in your blender or processor until smooth.

## 5. Inflammation Buster Smoothie

Ingredients:

-1 small pinch vanilla powder;

-1 tablespoon chia seeds;

-1 teaspoon turmeric, ground;

-1 teaspoon virgin coconut oil;

-1/2 teaspoon ginger, ground;

-1/2 teaspoon ground cinnamon;

-250 grams mango, chopped; and

-250 ml pure coconut milk.

Instructions:

-Blend everything in your blender or processor until smooth and creamy.

## 6. Raspberry Avocado Smoothie

Ingredients:

- 1 avocado, peeled and pitted

- ¾ cup raspberry juice

- ¾ cup orange juice

- ½ cup raspberries

Instructions:

- Blend the ingredients together in a blender, and enjoy!


## 7. Tomato Smoothie


This may not sound appetizing, but it really is quite delicious, and it is also an excellent way to get vitamins A, C, and K, as well as taking advantage of the ingredients' antioxidant and anti-inflammatory properties.

Ingredients:

- 2 cups tomatoes

- ¼ cup apple juice

- ½ cup tomato juice

- ¼ cup celery

- ½ cup carrots

- Hot sauce, to taste

- 2 cups ice

Instructions:

- Blend the ingredients in a blender, and enjoy!

## 8. Kale Smoothie

While kale makes a great base for smoothies, it can be difficult to get it into the right texture – sometimes the leaves ending up staying in bits that are a little too large to be appetizing. To avoid this, soak the kale leaves in water first for a few minutes.

Ingredients:

- 4 or 5 kale leaves
- 2 bananas
- 1 cup blueberries
- A few slices of cucumber

Instructions:

- Blend the ingredients in a blender until you have a smooth consistency.

## 9. Cherry Chocolate Shake

Ingredients:

- ½ cup frozen dark cherries, pitted
- 1 cup non-dairy milk (coconut, almond, or flax is best)
- 1 tablespoon unsweetened, unprocessed cocoa powder
- ½ teaspoon pure vanilla extract

- Several drops liquid stevia

- Ice cubes as desired

Instructions:

- Place all of the ingredients in a blender and blend until smooth.


## 10. Anti-Inflammatory Toddy

This recipe is fantastic because this toddy is very soothing and comforting, but it also has amazing anti-inflammatory properties thanks to the ginger, cinnamon, and turmeric that are used.

Ingredients:

- 1 cup cashew milk or almond milk

- ½ teaspoon ground turmeric

- ¼ teaspoon ground cinnamon

- ¼ teaspoon ground cardamom

- ¼ teaspoon freshly grated ginger

- Pinch of freshly cracked black pepper

- Pinch of vanilla powder

- 6 drops liquid stevia (optional, depending on sweet you would like this to be)

Instructions:

- In a small saucepan, heat the milk over medium heat for 2 to 3 minutes

- Add the spices, ginger, pepper, and vanilla, and stir to remove lumps

- Remove the mixture from the heat and pour it through a fine strainer to remove the grated ginger

- Add the stevia, if desired, and enjoy the drink served warm

# PART III: MAXIMIZING YOUR ANTI-INFLAMMATORY BENEFITS

# CHAPTER 6: EXERCISE

When the term "physical activity" is mentioned, we may automatically have thoughts of structured fitness routines like working out at the gym a couple of times weekly. While it's true that such activities play an important role for living healthy lifestyles, what we do outside of such fitness routines also impact our health.

Take for example that in the United States, the average person sits up to 10 hours daily. What's concerning is that studies have revealed that the effects of such a long period of daily inactivity can't be offset by working out even for 60 minutes at the end of the day. Personally, I've experienced this and I can say that we need to move continuously during the day to minimize the effects of such long, sedentary periods everyday. At the very least, I suggest getting up from our chairs every 50 minutes.

Brief periods of sitting here and there are but natural. But excessive sitting on a daily basis can have serious effects on our health over the long run and lead to a much shorter life expectancy. But getting up every 10 minutes isn't practical nor is keeping total sitting time to just 1 hour a day tops.

The next best thing is to walk more. Experts recommend taking at least 7 to 10 thousand daily, which you can monitor with free, downloadable apps that can track your steps. But for maximizing our anti-inflammatory health benefits, we'll need to incorporate a structured fitness routine or exercise program.

Studies have shown that a person is 47 percent less likely to have overly high levels of the messenger C-reactive protein (CRP) used in the inflammation process if that person exercises regularly, as compared to being sedentary. As discussed earlier in this book, CRP is a good indicator of chronic inflammation, so reduced levels of CRP indicate reduced amounts of inflammation.

As discussed in the diet chapter, weight loss may be something on which you need to focus as an overall health goal, but for the purposes of the Anti-Inflammatory Diet the focus is not on weight loss specifically. There is a substantial difference between exercising to lose weight and exercising to reduce chronic inflammation; exercising to reduce chronic inflammation focuses on getting the body healthy and strong, rather than on how many calories are being burned.

The most important thing to keep in mind when figuring out how to exercise to reduce chronic inflammation is that regular exercise tends to decrease inflammation, while 'acute' exercise (high energy when you are not used to it) can actually cause acute inflammation which could potentially lead to chronic inflammation. You must be careful to work your way into an exercise regime, rather than going full-steam ahead especially if you have not been particularly involved in exercise previously.

## EXERCISING FOR BATTLING INFLAMMATION

## HIGH INTENSITY INTERVAL TRAINING

Also known as HIIT, it's one of the best exercise routines for battling or managing chronic inflammation. It gives benefits that other, less strenuous exercises can't.

Recent studies link the anti-inflammatory benefits of HIIT to myokines, a type of proteins that produces signals in cells. Myokines are created by muscle fibers and can give significant metabolic syndrome protection, which is a group of conditions that include elevated blood sugar levels that increase our risks for cardio-vascular diseases and diabetes, among others.

It's been shown that HIIT can stimulate our muscles into effectively releasing the anti-inflammatory myokines. This in turn makes us more sensitive to insulin and more efficient in using glucose stored in our muscles. Myokines also assist in better metabolism of body fat within adipose tissues as well as within muscles (intra-muscular fat). As chemical messengers, myokines help minimize the release and effects of cytokines, which are inflammatory agents created by body fat.

One frequently asked question in terms of HIIT is the differences, if any, between high intensity cardio-vascular workouts and high intensity strength or weights training in terms of benefits. Generally speaking, both workouts can provide common benefits like improved muscle mass and strength, better cardiovascular fitness and better production of the so-called anti-aging and fitness hormone HGH or human growth hormone.

High intensity strength training however, provides better anti-inflammatory benefits. It's able to induce faster and deeper fatigue in muscles, which trigger the synthesis of important tissues and components that support them. These components include, among others, the anti-inflammatory agent myokines. So for battling chronic inflammation, high intensity strength training may be the best alternative.

# CHAPTER 7: REST AND RECUPERATION

But we also have to keep in mind that the saying "the more the merrier" doesn't really apply to regular exercise. In fact, too much exercise and very little rest can aggravate inflammation, among other things, instead of reducing it. To avoid or minimize chronic inflammation, regular exercise with adequate rest and recuperation periods are a must.

You may be a bit confused knowing that exercising can both cause and reduce inflammation. I understand. Here's a simpler way of understanding how exercise-inflammation relationship really goes, which isn't really complicated.

While it's true that exercise sessions, especially HIITs, can produce acute inflammation, this actually decreases the problematic chronic or systemic type of inflammation over the long haul. This is because the oxidative stress produced by regular exercising compels our bodies to fortify its antioxidant defense systems. Studies have shown that particular exercise programs can assist in reducing C-reactive protein, which is one of several inflammatory markers.

However, the acute type of inflammation from regular exercising can eventually turn chronic if proper rest and recuperation are not observed. As such, part of a regular exercise program must also include regularly adequate periods for recovery, which will help prevent the beneficial instances of acute inflammation from becoming harmful and chronic. Rest and recuperation is especially important

141

with HIIT because of the relatively higher stress it puts on our bodies.

Effective workout sessions basically give the body acute stress, which triggers powerful transitory but short-lived inflammatory response. Therefore, training or exercise programs that can effectively help in managing chronic inflammations involves lots of those acutely stressful workout sessions that with adequate amounts of rest and recuperation times in between, among others.

So what does "adequate" really mean? For one, different people are built differently so there's no hard and fast rule about that. However, one way to estimate if we're getting enough rest and recovery periods is by evaluating how we feel using the PRISH, particularly pain, injury or swelling. If we also get sick often, it's an indication that we're exercising too much and not getting enough rest and recuperation.

One good alternative – and potentially painless one at that – is the 48-hour guiding principle. Simply put, this means giving our muscles at least 48 hours of rest and recovery before subjecting them again to intense training. For example, if we worked out our chest muscles with HIIT today, the earliest we should be working them out again is after 2 days or on the 3rd day. Most bodybuilders and fitness experts abide by this principle.

Remember, the more isn't always merrier. And when it comes to maximizing the benefits of the Anti-Inflammatory Diet, we need to balance working out with enough rest and recuperation.

# CONCLUSION

Congratulations on having come this far and finishing the book. At this point, you've learned what inflammation really is, the difference between acute and chronic inflammation, the effects of the latter on our health, what we can do to prevent, minimize or even reverse chronic inflammation with the Anti-Inflammatory Diet, including the best foods to eat and a wide variety of delicious anti-inflammatory recipes. You've also learned a bit about what particular exercises can be beneficial for maximizing the benefits of the Anti-Inflammatory Diet, as well as the importance of giving yourself time to rest and recuperate so that you do not cause an inflammatory response in your body. You're now ready to kick some serious inflammatory butt.

However, knowing is just half the battle, as G.I. Joe would always say at the end of each episode back in the 1980s. The other half, which he doesn't say, is applying what we know. All these cool and fancy information and tactics about the Anti-Inflammation Diet will amount to nothing more than just trivia is we don't actually eat those foods – application! In this regard I highly encourage you to act immediately upon what you learned by trying at least 1 recipe each from the breakfast, lunch, dinner, desserts, snacks and shakes/smoothies within the week. The more you delay, the higher the chances you won't do anything about it. And when that happens, it's not me or anyone else who losses. It's you. So go ahead and give those delicious recipes a shot, you won't regret it.

Here's to your great health, my friend! Cheers!

20005557R00084

Printed in Great Britain
by Amazon